"*The 101 Coolest Simple Science Experiments* is a must-have book if you have kids or if you work with kids! This book really opens their minds to the wonderful world of science and gives them the chance to experiment, learn and have fun doing it!"

—Becky Mansfield, bestselling author of *Potty Train in a Weekend*

"No one makes science experiments more fun and easy than the moms behind Kids Activities Blog!"

—Megan Sheakoski, creator of Coffee Cups and Crayons

"Wow and amaze your kids (and even yourself) with these jaw dropping science experiments! There are so many ideas to do inside and outside with things you can find right at home. Be prepared for fun!"

—Cindy Hopper, founder of Skip to my Lou

"*The 101 Coolest Simple Science Experiments* is a must-have for all parents! The experiments are super fun, the instructions are really easy-to-follow and, most importantly, it provides hours of family-friendly entertainment! Your kids, and your child's teacher, will thank you!"

—Jenn Fishkind, founder of Princess Pinky Girl

"Holly Homer IS the kid's activities specialist! Millions rely on her to empower them with fun ideas for kids. Devour this book and make your little scientists happy!"

—Michael Stelzner, founder of My Kids' Adventures

"This book will give you ideas for a year's worth of weekends so you never have to hear 'I'm bored!' at your house."

—Angela England, author of *Gardening Like a Ninja*, founder of Untrained Housewife

"*The 101 Coolest Simple Science Experiments* makes science not only applicable to real life but encourages kids to have fun in the process! A must-have book."

—Mique Provost, author of *Make & Share Random Acts of Kindness*, founder of Thirty Handmade Days

"*The 101 Coolest Simple Science Experiments* is filled with smart activities that will keep everyone engaged in non-stop challenging fun!"

—Kelly Dixon, founder of Smart School House, author of *Smart School House Crafts for Kids*

"*The 101 Coolest Simple Science Experiments* is fabulous. It's the perfect gift for every parent or grandparent who wants to spend some fun, quality time with their children or grandchildren."

—Leigh Anne Wilkes, food and lifestyle blogger at Your Homebased Mom

"Science with the kids has never been so fun! Roll up your sleeves and get ready to see your little ones' faces light up!"

—Me Ra Koh, founder of The Photo Mom, Disney Junior host of "Capture Your Story with Me Ra Koh"

"*The 101 Coolest Simple Science Experiments* is not only the perfect resource for school science projects, it also provides a fantastic way to spend an afternoon having fun with your kids!"

—Stephanie Dulgarian, founder of Somewhat Simple, mother of 5

the
101

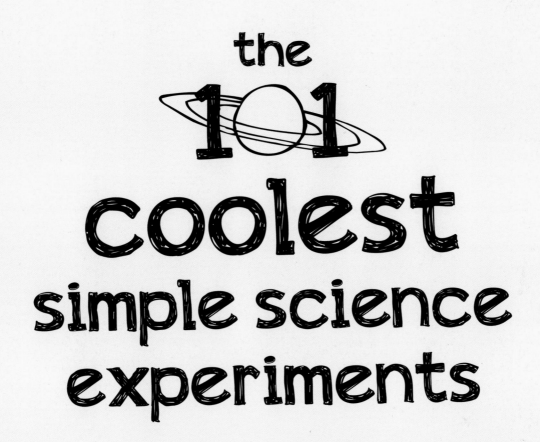

coolest
simple science
experiments

Rachel Miller,
Holly Homer &
Jamie Harrington

THE TEAM BEHIND KIDS ACTIVITIES BLOG
& THE QUIRKY MOMMA FACEBOOK PAGE

PAGE STREET
PUBLISHING CO.

PAGE STREET
PUBLISHING CO.

First published in 2016 by

Page Street Publishing Co.

27 Congress Street, Suite 103

Salem, MA 01970

www.pagestreetpublishing.com

Distributed by Macmillan, sales in Canada by The Canadian Manda Group.

19   18   17   16   1   2   3   4   5

ISBN-13: 978-1-62414-133-1

ISBN-10: 1-62414-133-1

Library of Congress Control Number: 2015954405

Cover and book design by Page Street Publishing Co.

Photography by Rachel Miller, Holly Homer and Jamie Harrington

Illustrations by Josh Manges

Printed and bound in China

Page Street is proud to be a member of 1% for the Planet. Members donate one percent of their sales to one or more of the over 1,500 environmental and sustainability charities across the globe who participate in this program.

To the greatest kids in the universe:
Lena, Ezra, Anya, Kora, Jonah, Noah, Ryan,
Reid, Rhett and Halle. We love you and are
grateful for the sense of wonder you
bring to our lives.

Contents

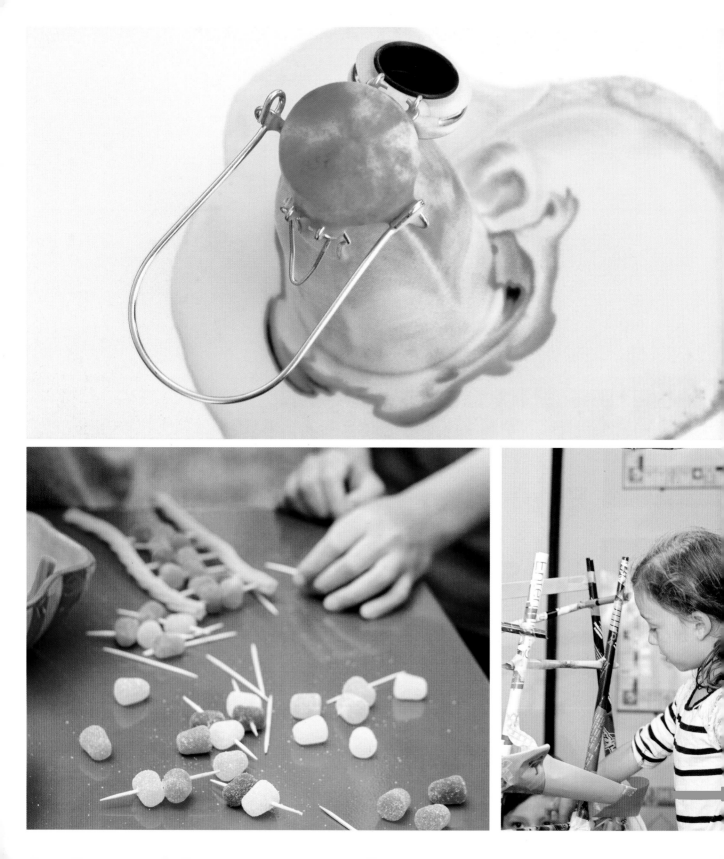

Introduction

Science is play.

It is the catalyst for curiosity that innately lives in the heart of a child. It is a safe area for the question WHY?

Asking why starts a wondrous adventure! And whys rarely travel alone. One why leads to another and before you know it you are leading a pack of whys down a path of playful discovery.

Being a scientist is fun. Laboratories are the ultimate playground, whether they are in a formal environment, in your backyard or on your kitchen table. They are where the whys come out to play!

There is no limit on playtime with whys. Whys are fine with playing for a few minutes, a few days or a lifetime.

Everyone can be a scientist. There is no age limit, IQ requirement or formal training required.

Let's investigate!

Rachel Miller   *Holly Homer*

Jamie Harrington

Chapter 1

Kitchen Chemistry

The kitchen is the ultimate laboratory. Ordinary ingredients are transformed by chemical reactions. These things happen every day in the kitchen, but their magic often goes unnoticed.

Holly's pick: Exploding Baggies (page 22) is one of my kids' favorite experiments. Living in a household with three boys has given me an appreciation for anything that explodes.

Rachel's pick: I think the Creeping Ink (page 21) is terrific. Your kids will be mesmerized, as mine were, creating one-of-a kind shirts— with science!

Jamie's pick: Bursting Soap Cloud (page 12) is my favorite science experiment of all time. I like washing my hands with it after!

Bursting Soap Cloud

MESS METER: 4   ADULT SUPERVISION REQUIRED   SAFETY PRECAUTIONS

PREP TIME: 1 MINUTE
EXPERIMENT DURATION: 2 MINUTES

Supplies Needed
- ☐ Bar of Ivory soap
- ☐ Microwave-safe dish

Science Question:
What happens to gases as they are heated?

Charles's Law (named after a scientist, Jacques Charles) says gases expand when they're heated. We can watch Charles's Law in action with a bar of Ivory soap in the microwave.

The Experiment

Unwrap the bar of soap and place it on the microwave-safe dish. Microwave the soap for 1½ to 2 minutes, watching closely to see what happens. (This won't hurt your microwave, we promise!) Let the soap cool a bit and remove it from the microwave.

Why It Worked

When you heat up the Ivory soap, you get to see Charles's Law—the air inside the soap expands when it's heated. The soap puffs up as the air trapped inside gets bigger.

The Outcome

When you microwave Ivory soap, it expands as much as six times in size and feels brittle and flaky. Try washing your hands with it.

Safety First!

The soap will be very hot when you pull it out of the microwave. Be sure to let it cool.

Tip

This experiment won't work with other brands of soap, because they aren't as porous as Ivory.

Did You Know?

October 15th is Global Hand-Washing Day. It's a good idea to wash your hands the other 364 days of the year too, though.

Dancing Candy

MESS
METER: 1

ADULT
SUPERVISION
REQUIRED

SAFETY
PRECAUTIONS

PREP TIME: 10 MINUTES
EXPERIMENT DURATION: 2 MINUTES

Supplies Needed

☐ Saucepan
☐ Water
☐ Rainbow-colored hard candies

Science Question:
How does water boil?

We can see what happens to water molecules as heat or energy is introduced to the pan.

The Experiment

Fill a saucepan with water and have an adult put it on the stove to boil. When the water warms up a bit, add a few pieces of candy and watch as the water starts to boil. At first, it looks like nothing is happening, but watch closely!

The Outcome

The water starts to boil and your candies bounce all around the saucepan.

Why It Worked

As the water heats up, it expands and tiny bubbles form from gas in the water. The super cool color waves around your candy are from the light being bent as it passes through the steam. When the big bubbles show up you're actually changing the liquid (water) to a gas (steam)!

Variation

• Boil two pots of water, one full of cold and the other full of hot. Which one boils first?

Did You Know?

Roughly three-quarters of your body is made of water. That's almost the whole thing!

Safety First!

Boiling water is VERY hot and so is the stove. Make sure you have a parent close by when you're watching your pot.

Carbon Dioxide Balloons

MESS
METER: 1

NO ADULT
SUPERVISION
REQUIRED

PREP TIME: 10 MINUTES
EXPERIMENT DURATION: 5 MINUTES

Supplies Needed

- ☐ Spoon
- ☐ 2 teaspoons (10 g) baking soda
- ☐ Balloon
- ☐ ⅓ cup (90 ml) white vinegar
- ☐ Old water bottle

Science Question:

Can you combine a liquid and a solid to make a gas?

Baking soda is a solid and vinegar is a liquid, but when you mix the two together it creates a whole new substance: gas.

The Experiment

Using the spoon, put the baking soda into the balloon.

Pour the vinegar into the bottle until it's about one-third full. Keeping the baking soda in the body of the balloon, stretch the mouth over the bottle's opening. Then dump the baking soda from the balloon into the bottle.

The Outcome

As the vinegar and baking soda mix, a gas—carbon dioxide— is created. It is a by-product of vinegar and baking soda reacting together, and the balloon blows up.

Why It Worked

The vinegar is acetic acid, and the baking soda is a base—the opposite pH to an acid. When they mix, it causes a reaction and carbonic acid is formed, separating into bubbles of carbon dioxide (CO_2) and water. The CO_2 has nowhere to go except up into the balloon, causing it to inflate.

Variation

- Change the temperature of your vinegar, making it hotter or colder, and see if that affects the speed at which your balloon grows.

Try This!

Bounce your balloon. Does it bounce as easily as a regular air-filled balloon? The CO_2 gas is heavier than air. Helium is lighter than air, making balloons filled with that gas float.

Did You Know?

Vinegar has no expiration date. It never "goes bad."

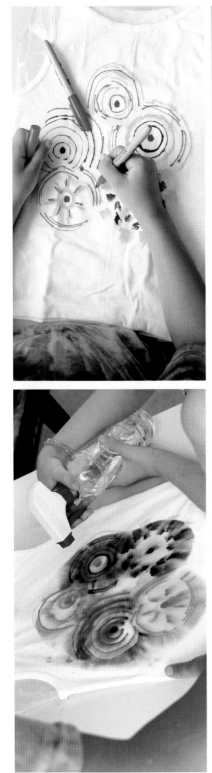

Dissolving Ink

MESS
METER: 3

ADULT
SUPERVISION
REQUIRED

PREP TIME: 10 MINUTES
EXPERIMENT DURATION: 20 MINUTES
PLUS DRYING TIME

Supplies Needed

- ☐ Spray bottle
- ☐ 70% rubbing alcohol
- ☐ Aluminum foil or cardboard to line the inside of the shirt
- ☐ White T-shirt
- ☐ Colored permanent markers

Science Question:
Can you make permanent ink dissolve?

A solvent can break the bond of a permanent marker, freeing the ink to spread and burst.

The Experiment

Fill the spray bottle with rubbing alcohol. Cut your foil and put it inside the shirt to keep your marker from bleeding through. Color your shirt with the markers and spray the shirt with alcohol.

The Outcome

Watch as the colors morph into a colorful explosion!

Why It Worked

The alcohol acts as a solvent and dissolves the ink as it saturates the shirt, causing the ink to spread.

Variations

- If you don't have an old shirt to spare, this same technique can be used on paper towels or coffee filters.

- Try hydrogen peroxide or water and see how the colors change (or don't!).

Tip

After your shirt is dry, wash it alone so the colors don't bleed onto the rest of your laundry.

Did You Know?

Way back in 12th century BC, the Chinese used ink from squids to write and draw with.

Rising Raisins

MESS
METER: 1

NO ADULT
SUPERVISION
REQUIRED

PREP TIME: 2 MINUTES
EXPERIMENT DURATION: 5 TO 20 MINUTES

Supplies Needed

☐ A handful of raisins
☐ 1 clear glass of water
☐ 1 clear glass of soda

Science Question:
Why does a raisin rise in soda, but sink in water?

Even though a glass of water and a glass of clear soda look the same, raisins react very differently due to buoyancy.

The Experiment

Add 5 raisins to each glass and watch what happens.

The Outcome

The raisins in the water will stay at the bottom of the glass, but the raisins in the soda will rise to the top.

Just for Fun

You can make your own raisins by placing grapes on a paper plate on a sunny windowsill or by spreading them onto a cookie sheet in a warm (lowest setting) oven for 24 hours.

Why It Worked

Raisins sink in water (and initially in the soda) because they are denser than the liquid. The soda's carbon dioxide molecules stick to the wrinkles of the raisins, causing them to have increased buoyancy and rise. When the bubbles pop or the raisin gets soggy, it will start to sink again.

Variations

• If you're prepared for a mess, try dropping a whole handful of raisins into a glass of soda.

• You can try heating up your soda or making it very cold, too!

Creeping Ink

PREP TIME: 5 MINUTES
EXPERIMENT DURATION: 7 MINUTES

Supplies Needed

- ☐ Cup
- ☐ Water
- ☐ Tablespoon measure
- ☐ 70% rubbing alcohol
- ☐ Coin
- ☐ Coffee filter
- ☐ Black marker
- ☐ Rubber band

Science Question:
What colors are in black?

Chromatography is a way to separate compounds so they can be seen individually.

The Experiment

Fill the cup with water to about 1 inch (2.5 cm) from the top. Add 1 tablespoon (15 ml) of rubbing alcohol to the cup. Place the coin in the middle of the coffee filter and trace a thick line around it with your marker. Drape the coffee filter over the cup so that the filter just touches the water. Secure it to the cup with the rubber band. Watch as the water creeps up the coffee filter.

The Outcome

As the water moves up the fibers of the coffee filter, it separates the pigments in the marker ink into their components.

Why It Worked

The lighter particles of ink travel the fastest and farthest, and the heavier color pigments are slower to move.

Can you tell how many colors are in the black pen?

Variation

- Try different brands of black markers. Different companies use different combinations to get black!

Tip

Do this experiment faster by increasing the amount of rubbing alcohol in your water.

Exploding Baggies

MESS
METER: 5

ADULT
SUPERVISION
REQUIRED

PREP TIME: 5 MINUTES
EXPERIMENT DURATION: 2 MINUTES

Supplies Needed
- ⅓ cup (80 ml) white vinegar
- 1 zipper-lock bag
- 10 drops of food coloring (optional)
- Clothespin
- 2 tablespoons (28 g) baking soda

Science Question:
What takes up more space, a solid and a liquid, or a gas?

Combine a solid and a liquid to see if the resulting chemical reaction is bigger than the components by themselves.

The Experiment

Pour the vinegar into the bag and add a few drops of food coloring. Twist the plastic above the liquid, and hold the twist secure with a clothespin. Now, above the clothespin, add the baking soda and close the bag's zipper.

Take off the clothespin and let the vinegar drop into the bag. Shake it and watch the reaction!

The Outcome

The bag blows up like a balloon.

Why It Worked

When baking soda and vinegar mix together, it causes a reaction that creates gas. Gas molecules take up more space than the liquid and the solid do, which is why the bag expands.

Tip

Do this in an easy-to-clean location. We suggest outside with a hose handy—or maybe in the bathtub!

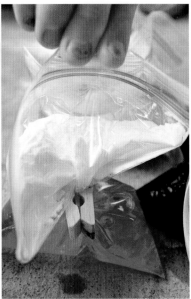

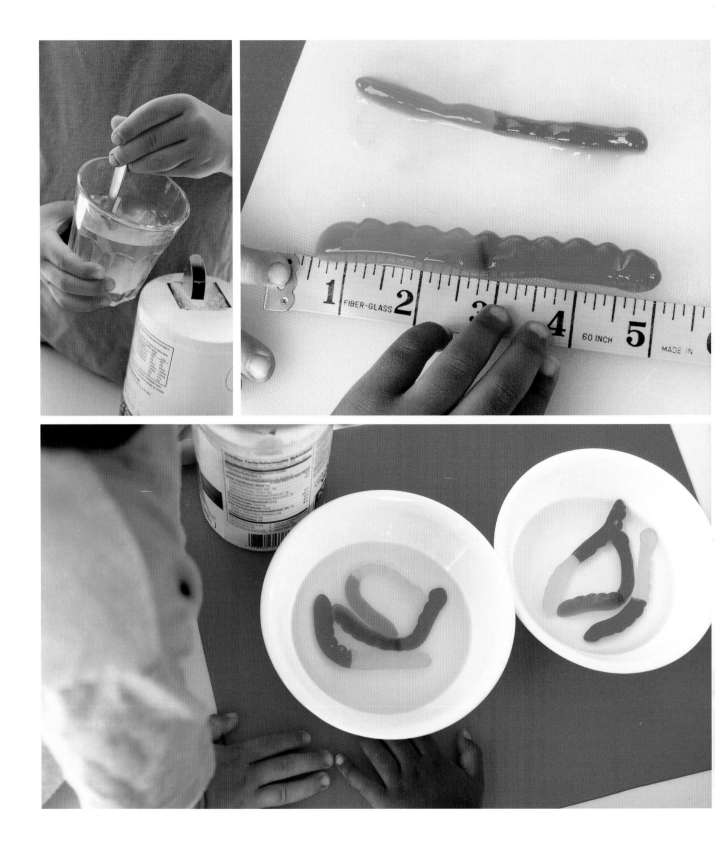

Grow Giant Worms

MESS METER: 3

NO ADULT SUPERVISION REQUIRED

PREP TIME: 2 MINUTES
EXPERIMENT DURATION: 2–3 HOURS

Supplies Needed
- ☐ Ruler
- ☐ 6 gummy worms
- ☐ Paper and pencil
- ☐ 2 glass bowls
- ☐ ⅔ cup (160 ml) warm water
- ☐ ¼ teaspoon salt
- ☐ Spoon

Science Question:
Is it easier for your body to absorb plain or salt water?

Most of the water on our planet is salt water, yet we don't drink it. Let's use gummy worms to show how different types of water are absorbed by our body.

The Experiment

With the ruler, measure the length of the gummy worms. Write this on a piece of paper. In a bowl, combine ⅓ cup (80 ml) of the water and the salt, and mix together with a spoon. Add the remaining ⅓ cup (80 ml) water to the other bowl. Write which bowl is which on a piece of paper and place under the bowl. Put 3 gummy worms in each bowl. Let the worms sit in the bowls for a couple of hours.

Pull out the worms and measure them again. Are your worms bigger?

The Outcome

The gummy worms in both bowls absorbed water. However, the worms in the plain water absorbed more water and grew much larger than the worms in the salt water.

Why It Worked

When gummy worms are added to water, the water molecules move through the tiny holes in the surface of the candy. The gelatin keeps the gummy worms from dissolving.

Critical Thinking

Plain water is easier for our bodies to absorb. That's why we don't drink salt water.

Variation

- Try different liquids. Will your gummy worms dissolve in soda or orange juice? What about if you heat your water or put it in the refrigerator first?

Did You Know?

Gummy bears were invented 60 years before the gummy worm, and July 15 is National Gummy Worm Day.

Glow Cups

MESS
METER: 2

ADULT
SUPERVISION
REQUIRED

PREP TIME: 5 MINUTES
EXPERIMENT DURATION: 5 MINUTES

Supplies Needed

- ☐ Tonic water
- ☐ 2 clear plastic cups
- ☐ Black light
- ☐ Pliers
- ☐ Neon yellow highlighter

Science Question:
How do glow-in-the-dark products work?

A lot of things that glow in the dark do so because they contain chemicals called quinine and pyranine. These chemicals absorb light and create a new wave of light at a lower wavelength, creating a cool glow.

The Experiment

Pour tonic water in one of the cups and turn off the lights. Now shine a black light onto your cup. What do you see?

Fill the other cup with tap water and use pliers to take the bottom off the highlighter. Pull out the ink tube and drop it into the cup. The ink will bleed into the water and make it change color. Now, shine the black light on the water. Whoa!

The Outcome

The black light makes your water glow. The tonic water will be blue, and the marker water will glow whatever color your highlighter is.

Why It Worked

Tonic water contains the chemical quinine that glows a blue color and the highlighter ink contains the fluorescein chemical pyranine. You can't see these chemicals, but when the black light hits them, the light is converted into a new form that you can see! That's what makes it glow.

Variation

- Make Jell-O with tonic water for a glow-in-the-dark dessert!

Tip

If you can't get your highlighter water to glow, cut off the plastic tubing.

Did You Know?

Some scorpions glow bright blue under a black light. Scientists aren't sure why they glow, but they know it happens because of a chemical called betacarabine in the scorpion's back.

Circular Diffusion

MESS
METER: 3

ADULT
SUPERVISION
REQUIRED

PREP TIME: 5 TO 10 MINUTES
EXPERIMENT DURATION: OVERNIGHT

Supplies Needed

- ☐ 2 cups (470 ml) water
- ☐ Microwave-safe bowl
- ☐ 3 packages of plain gelatin
- ☐ Spoon
- ☐ Cookie sheet
- ☐ Straw
- ☐ Food coloring

Science Question:
What is diffusion?

When molecules move from a place where there are lots of molecules and spread out to a much larger space where there are fewer molecules, that's called diffusion.

The Experiment

Pour the water into a microwave-safe bowl and have a parent microwave it until the water is boiling, and then carefully remove the bowl with oven mitts. Pour in all 3 packages of gelatin. Stir with a spoon until dissolved. Pour your mixture onto a cookie sheet and let it harden overnight.

Take your straw and poke holes in the gelatin mixture about 3 inches (7.5 cm) apart. Drop 2 or 3 drops of food coloring into each hole and let it sit for 2 to 3 hours.

Why It Worked

This is diffusion, when the food coloring spreads from one place to over a larger area.

Variation

- Add glitter to your mix or use cookie cutters to make gelatin window clings!

The Outcome

The food coloring spreads out in a perfect circle around each hole.

Did You Know?

In the early 1900s immigrants were offered Jell-O when they moved to the United States as a "Welcome to America" gift.

Ice Cream in a Can

PREP TIME: 10 MINUTES
EXPERIMENT DURATION: 20 TO 30 MINUTES

Supplies Needed

- ☐ 1 cup (235 ml) whipping cream
- ☐ ½ teaspoon vanilla extract
- ☐ 2 tablespoons (25 g) sugar
- ☐ Small coffee can with lid
- ☐ Spoon
- ☐ Packing tape
- ☐ Large coffee can with lid
- ☐ 4 cups (800 g) ice
- ☐ ½ cup (145 g) kosher salt

Science Question:
Can you speed up the process of changing a liquid to a solid?

In this experiment, we will see how salt makes it quicker and easier to freeze things by making the ice super cold. We are making ice cream.

The Experiment

Pour the cream, vanilla and sugar into the small coffee can, stir with the spoon and seal the lid with the tape.

Place the smaller can inside the large coffee can. Fill the space between the two cans with ice and then salt. Tape the lid on the larger can and roll the can. After 30 minutes has passed, remove the lid from the large can, remove and rinse off the small can and then open it.

The Outcome

You get ice cream!

Try This!

Fill one ice cube tray or plastic container with plain water and fill another with a salt water solution. Put them in the freezer. Which do you think will freeze first?

Why It Worked

When you mix ice and salt, the ice becomes even colder than normal, making it perfect to freeze even moving liquid, like the cream in the can. Because it freezes so quickly, the ice cream has crystals of ice dispersed between the cream, and doesn't freeze into a solid block.

Variation

- Try to make ice cream in zipper-lock bags instead of cans. Pour the ingredients into a quart-size zipper-lock bag. Double bag it with a larger gallon-size freezer bag. Fill the big bag with ice and salt. Gently shake the bag until your ice cream forms.

Did You Know?

Vanilla is the most popular flavor of ice cream.

Secret Mirror Messages

MESS
METER: 2

NO ADULT
SUPERVISION
REQUIRED

PREP TIME: 10 TO 15 MINUTES
EXPERIMENT DURATION: 5 MINUTES

Supplies Needed

- ☐ Cotton swab
- ☐ Dish soap
- ☐ Paper towel

Science Question:
How do you keep steam from fogging up a mirror?

In this experiment you can see the effects of a water-hating (or hydrophobic) substance when water that has become a gas (or steam) hits it.

The Experiment

Dip the cotton swab into the soap and blot the swab onto the towel so nothing drips. Use the cotton swab to write a message on the mirror.

Take a hot shower—hot enough to fill the room with steam. Check out the mirror.

The Outcome

Your words and drawings show through the steam.

Why It Worked

When you take a hot shower, the mirror in your bathroom gets covered in a thin layer of steam. The droplets of water from the steam attached to the mirror, making it appear "foggy." But, when you wrote on the mirror with soap, the soap prevented the water from clinging to that part of the mirror.

Critical Thinking

Water loves to stick to things. This is why your skin feels clammy when it's raining outside, even if you're under an umbrella.

Try This!

To keep a mirror from fogging up, fill a spray bottle half with water and half with vinegar. Add a drop or two of dishwashing soap and spray the mirror. Wipe clean with a paper towel. No more fog!

Lava Lamp

MESS
METER: 4

ADULT
SUPERVISION
REQUIRED

PREP TIME: 10 MINUTES
EXPERIMENT DURATION: 10 MINUTES

Supplies Needed

- ☐ Clear container or bottle
- ☐ Vegetable oil
- ☐ Water
- ☐ 10 drops food coloring (red is best)
- ☐ Small cup
- ☐ Knife
- ☐ Effervescent or fizzing tablets, such as Alka-Seltzer

Science Question:
How does gas behave in a liquid?

Have you ever seen a lava lamp? They are groovy! Gobs of wax move through lit water. Here we will use science to create our own wax-less lava lamp!

The Experiment

Fill the bottle three-fourths full with oil. Mix some water and food coloring together in a small cup and add some of the colored water to the oil bottle, leaving 1 to 2 inches (2.5 to 5 cm) of air space at the top of the bottle. Watch for a few minutes while the oil and water separate.

Have a parent use the knife to cut the tablet into three or four pieces. Drop one piece into the mixture and watch what happens. To keep the effect going, add another piece or two.

The Outcome

As you watch, colorful blobs of water will rise and fall through the oil.

Why It Worked

Oil is made up of non-polar molecules, but water is pure polar molecules. No matter how hard you might shake oil and water together, they will never mix. Oil also rises to the top of the bottle. This is because water is denser than oil.

The tablet, after being dropped into the bottle, begins to dissolve and creates gas bubbles. As the bubbles rise, they take a bit of the colored water along with them to the surface. When the blob of water reaches the top, the gas escapes. Down goes the water.

Variation

- For an even greater lava lamp effect, you can shine a flashlight through the bottom of the bottle.

Did You Know?

A British accountant named Edward Craven Walker created the first lava lamp. He called them "Astro Lamps."

Marshmallow Molecules

MESS
METER: 3

ADULT
SUPERVISION
REQUIRED

SAFETY
PRECAUTIONS

PREP TIME: 5 MINUTES
EXPERIMENT DURATION: 15+ MINUTES

Supplies Needed

- ☐ 6 large marshmallows (we used Peeps)
- ☐ Glass bowl
- ☐ Spoon
- ☐ 1 tablespoon (15 ml) melted butter or coconut oil
- ☐ 1 cup (120 g) powdered sugar

Science Question:

What can cause the space between molecules to expand (grow) and contract (shrink)?

Often we can't see molecules moving. In this experiment we will watch molecules expand and contract in marshmallows.

The Experiment

Observe the size of the marshmallows, then place them in a bowl and heat in the microwave for 15 to 25 seconds, until the marshmallows have doubled in size. See how the marshmallows expanded with the heat?

Now push on the marshmallows with the spoon and watch them deflate with the pressure.

Add the butter or coconut oil to the melted marshmallows and stir it up. Spoon in the powdered sugar using just enough to create a non-sticky dough consistency.

The Outcome

You now have edible play dough that is a treat!

Why It Worked

Heat is energy and will cause the molecules in the marshmallows to move faster, expanding the space between them. As the molecules are compressed by stirring and cooling, the space contracts or gets smaller.

Variation

- Place a marshmallow in the freezer for a few hours. Can you guess what will happen to it?

Safety First!

The mashmallows will be very hot and sticky when you pull them out of the microwave. Do not touch them!

Did You Know?

The first marshmallows were made from the sap of the marsh mallow plant, and people have been eating marshmallows for thousands of years.

Soda Eruption

PREP TIME: 2 MINUTES
EXPERIMENT DURATION: 2 MINUTES

Supplies Needed

- ☐ 2-liter plastic bottle of diet soda (any soda works, but a diet soda won't leave a sticky mess)
- ☐ Mentos mints

Science Question: What happens when a gas is released from a liquid?

The three states of matter are liquid, gas and solid. In this experiment we will see what happens when you release the gas from a liquid.

The Experiment

Put your bottle on the ground outdoors, and have a hose handy—this is messy. Open the bottle and drop in 2 Mentos.

The Outcome

A geyser of liquid will shoot out of the bottle.

Why It Worked

Soda is made by dissolving carbon dioxide (CO_2) into liquid, usually by pressure. But CO_2 is nonpolar and water is polar. That means they don't like to stay mixed. When the mint is dropped into the soda, it falls to the bottom and carbon dioxide bubbles are freed from the soda. Because the bubbles are lighter than soda, they rise to the surface of the soda—FAST, like in a geyser.

Did You Know?

The average American drinks 44 gallons (167 liters) of soda in a year.

Variation

- Try changing up one of the ingredients in this experiment. You can either use a different type of candy, a different brand of soda or even change the temperature of the soda. How do these changes affect the "geyser"?

Plastic Milk

MESS
METER: 4

ADULT
SUPERVISION
REQUIRED

PREP TIME: 15 MINUTES, PLUS 30 MINUTES COOLING TIME
EXPERIMENT DURATION: 5 MINUTES

Supplies Needed

- ☐ 1 cup (235 ml) whole milk
- ☐ Mug
- ☐ Cup
- ☐ Food coloring (optional)
- ☐ 4 teaspoons (20 ml) white vinegar
- ☐ Spoon
- ☐ Scrap of fabric
- ☐ Rubber band

Science Question:
Can you make milk solid without freezing it?

Creating a sort of plastic from common kitchen ingredients is a great way to watch molecules rearrange themselves right before your eyes.

The Experiment

Pour the milk into the mug and heat in the microwave for a minute or two. You want the milk to be hot, but not boiling.

In a separate cup, combine the food coloring and the vinegar. Stir with a spoon. Pour the vinegar into the hot milk. Watch the milk curdle and clumps form as you stir the ingredients together.

After the milk has curdled strain the curds, pouring the liquid out. We used the fabric and the rubber band to make a strainer. After the curds cool, about 30 minutes, smush this plastic-like substance into a shape, like a ball.

The Outcome

You will get blobs of a plastic-like substance.

Why It Worked

You can find a protein called "casein" in milk. When you add an acid (like vinegar) to the casein, it causes the proteins to clump together so the liquid can be poured off. Those are the blobs in the milk, and they are like plastic.

Did You Know?

Buttons in the early 19th century were made with this type of plastic. People "wore" their milk!

Missing Ingredient Sleuth

MESS
METER: 2

ADULT
SUPERVISION
REQUIRED

PREP TIME: 10 MINUTES
EXPERIMENT DURATION: 1 HOUR OR MORE

Supplies Needed

☐ Your favorite cookie recipe
☐ Enough ingredients to double the recipe

Science Question:

Have you ever baked cookies and wondered whether you really need every single ingredient?

Baking is chemistry! Check out how just one ingredient can drastically change the way a cookie looks or tastes.

The Experiment

With an adult, assemble most of the ingredients for your doubled recipe, leaving out the eggs, baking powder and butter. Separate into four different bowls.

The goal is to leave out just one ingredient from each portion—one bowl will be without eggs, another without baking powder, the third without butter; the fourth will have all ingredients, making it a normal cookie recipe.

Add the other non-excluded ingredients to each bowl and bake according to the recipe.

The Outcome

When you leave out even just one ingredient, your favorite cookie recipe turns out different. Each ingredient is important! Leaving out eggs, baking powder or butter can change the results dramatically in the way the cookie tastes, feels or looks.

Why It Worked

Each ingredient plays a special role in the cookie recipe's chemistry. The ingredients all work together. Baking powder helps the batter rise so the cookies aren't flat disks. Butter gives the cookie texture and tenderness. Eggs do a lot of different things in a recipe. They help the batter bind together, rise when baked and give the baked cookie a lovely toasty color.

Variation

• If you leave out vanilla, it won't change the structure of the cookies, but it will change the flavor and smell. If you leave out flour, your cookies will lack structure and be a gooey mess. If you leave out the sugar, you might complain about the taste!

Did You Know?

Americans on average eat almost one cookie per day!

Popcorn on the Cob

PREP TIME: 1 MINUTE
EXPERIMENT DURATION: 5 MINUTES

Supplies Needed

- ☐ Dried corn still on the cob
- ☐ 1 teaspoon (5 ml) canola oil
- ☐ Paper lunch sack

Science Question:
Can you pop corn that is still on the cob?

Using a cob of dried corn, you are going to make microwave popcorn!

The Experiment

Place your corncob and oil into the paper bag and fold down the top. Cook in the microwave for 2 to 4 minutes. Listen for the pops to slow down.

Why It Worked

A tiny bit of moisture is in every kernel of popcorn. When the kernel is heated, the moisture turns to steam and expands, causing a mini explosion.

The Outcome

You made popcorn! It will pop right off the cob.

Idea

If you can't find dried popcorn, don't worry—you can use any corn on the cob to make your own. Just boil it in hot water for 5 minutes and then bake in the oven at 200°F (100°C) for 3 to 4 hours. Dried popcorn can store for up to 12 months!

Did You Know?

Microwave popcorn was first invented in 1981 and had to be stored in the freezer.

Mixing Oil and Water

MESS METER: 2

NO ADULT SUPERVISION REQUIRED

PREP TIME: 3 MINUTES
EXPERIMENT DURATION: 3 TO 30 MINUTES

Supplies Needed

- ☐ White casserole dish
- ☐ Cooking oil (enough to completely cover the bottom of the dish at least ½ inch [1.3 cm] deep)
- ☐ Liquid food coloring
- ☐ Whisk
- ☐ Broken egg yolk

Science Question: Can oil and water mix?

Everyone knows that oil and water don't mix, but when you put them in the right company they can be combined.

The Experiment

Fill the bottom of the dish with oil and whisk in a few drops of food coloring. The oil and the coloring (which is mainly water) will not mix. The drops of food coloring may get smaller and smaller, but they are still separate from the oil. Let the liquid sit for a few minutes. The drops of food coloring will grow back together into bigger blobs.

Add 2 teaspoons (10 ml) of egg yolk to the oil and food coloring mixture and whisk it again.

The Outcome

Your oil and water will now mix into a cloudy concoction.

Why It Worked

Oil and water don't mix well together. Oil is hydrophobic, which means its molecules repel water. Water is hydrophilic, meaning it loves itself and will mix with other hydrophilic liquids. The egg yolk contains a fatty substance that acts as an emulsifier. An emulsifier can combine these two liquids that are usually unmixable.

Did You Know?

Most eggs have a single yolk. But some eggs have two! The chances of getting a double-yolk egg is 0.1 percent.

Orange Float

PREP TIME: 5 MINUTES
EXPERIMENT DURATION: 5 MINUTES

Supplies Needed

- ☐ 2 oranges
- ☐ Scale
- ☐ Clear plastic or glass bowl
- ☐ Water

Science Question:
Can you make an orange float?

If you drop an orange into water, will it float? Definitely not! But could you do something to an orange to make it float? In this experiment, you will find out!

The Experiment

Pick two oranges that are roughly the same weight and peel one and leave the other with its peel on. Put both oranges on the scale and weigh them. The one with the peel should be heavier.

Fill the bowl with water. Drop in the peeled orange. Next, drop in the unpeeled orange.

The Outcome

The peeled orange should have sunk like a rock to the bottom of your bowl, while the unpeeled orange floats.

Why It Worked

The unpeeled orange floated because the orange rind is actually filled with tiny pockets of air, making it buoyant. Even though the unpeeled orange is heavier than the peeled one, it floats!

Variation

- Try this with other fruits. Can you make a lemon float? How about a grapefruit? An apple?

Try This!

Next time you are in a pool, try to make yourself more buoyant by puffing yourself up with air and floating on your back.

Did You Know?

It is easier to carry something heavy in the pool. This is called the Archimedes' Principle. The object will feel lighter because the displaced water applies pressure against the object, carrying it with you.

Magic Potion

MESS
METER: 5

ADULT
SUPERVISION
REQUIRED

PREP TIME: 5 MINUTES
EXPERIMENT DURATION: 5 MINUTES

Supplies Needed

- ☐ 1 cup (235 ml) 3% hydrogen peroxide
- ☐ ¼ cup (60 ml) bubble solution
- ☐ Tall bottle or vase
- ☐ Food coloring
- ☐ Cup
- ☐ ¼ cup (60 ml) warm water
- ☐ 1 tablespoon (9 g) active dry yeast (or 1 packet)
- ☐ Spoon
- ☐ A place to be messy

Science Question:
What happens when chemicals break down?

According to the law of thermodynamics, chemical compositions eventually fall apart. With hydrogen peroxide we can watch the molecules break down. All we need is a catalyst—yeast.

The Experiment

Pour the hydrogen peroxide and bubble solution into your tall bottle. Add a LOT of drops of food coloring (at least 15 drops). In a separate cup, mix the warm water and the yeast and stir with a spoon. Once the yeast is dissolved into the water, pour the yeast mixture into the bottle and stand back and watch!

The Outcome

A ton of bubbles emerge from the bottle.

Why It Worked

The yeast is a catalyst. It will break down the hydrogen peroxide. The bubble solution thickens the surface tension, capturing the escaping oxygen in lots and lots of frothy bubbles.

Variations

- Replace the 3% hydrogen peroxide with an 8% solution for a bigger reaction. You may be able to find these at your local beauty supply store.

- If you want a less-mess version, consider sprinkling some yeast in the bottom of a dish, add a couple of drops of food coloring, and pour a couple of tablespoons of hydrogen peroxide over the yeast. You will experience the experiment on a smaller scale.

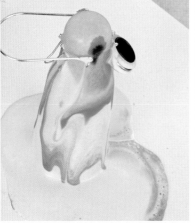

Did You Know?

Water is also a mixture of the hydrogen (2 atoms) and oxygen (1 atom) and is a relatively stable chemical. Unlike water, hydrogen peroxide has two oxygen atoms, making it less stable than water.

Idea

Try having an adult light a match over the potion as it is bubbling out of the bottle. Listen closely: what do you hear?

Red Glowing Spinach

PREP TIME: 15 MINUTES
EXPERIMENT DURATION: 5 MINUTES

Supplies Needed

- ☐ A large handful of spinach
- ☐ Saucepan
- ☐ Water
- ☐ Tongs
- ☐ Blender
- ☐ 1 tablespoon (15 ml) vegetable oil
- ☐ Fine-mesh strainer
- ☐ Bowl
- ☐ Black light

Science Question:
Is chlorophyll always green?

Did you know chlorophyll doesn't always look green? In this experiment, you'll use spinach to find out what color it can also look.

The Experiment

First we need to extract the chlorophyll from the spinach. Boil the leaves in a saucepan of water for 1 minute. Take the spinach out of the water with tongs and put it in the blender with the vegetable oil. Blend until smooth.

Strain the green liquid through a fine-mesh strainer into the bowl. The leaf goo will stay in the strainer, and the green chlorophyll-infused oil will fall into the bowl. Shine the black light onto the green liquid.

Why It Worked

Boiling the spinach pulls the chlorophyll, which is used by the plant to capture sunlight, out of the spinach cells. Chlorophyll absorbs all wavelengths of visible light—except green. Plants look green because the leaves don't absorb the green light, so it is reflected back to us. When you shine a black light at the spinach slush, the chlorophyll absorbs the UV light and you see a bright red color.

The Outcome

The chlorophyll in plants looks green under normal light, but it glows red under UV light, such as a black light!

Did You Know?

In the 1930s Americans bought 33 percent more spinach because of the cartoon *Popeye*!

Just for Fun

Did you notice how much the spinach shrank when cooked it? Guess how much fresh spinach would be needed to end up with ½ cup (90 g) of cooked spinach.

Salty Ice

PREP TIME: 5 MINUTES, PLUS OVERNIGHT TO FREEZE
(IF DOING VARIATION)
EXPERIMENT DURATION: 30 TO 40 MINUTES

Supplies Needed

- ☐ Blocks and cubes of frozen ice
- ☐ Large bowl
- ☐ Salt
- ☐ Droppers
- ☐ Food coloring

Science Question:

What happens to salty water when you try to freeze it?

Salt affects the temperature at which water freezes. We will see how salt affects the freezing rate in this experiment.

The Experiment

Place the ice in a large bowl. Sprinkle the salt over the ice. Using droppers, squirt food coloring over the melting pits left by the salt.

Why It Worked

When you sprinkle the salt on the ice, the ice starts to melt. The salt makes it harder for the water molecules to form ice crystals. The freezing point of water lowers as more salt is added.

The Outcome

The food coloring will help you see the effects of the melting more clearly.

Variation

- Fill two identical plastic containers halfway with warm water. Add salt (⅓ cup [75 g]) to one of the containers and stir. Place both containers in the freezer and check them every few hours. Which container froze first, the salt-filled one or the one with just tap water?

Did You Know?

This is why you sprinkle salt on sidewalks in winter to melt the ice. Tap water freezes at 32°F (0°C), but salt water freezes at about 15°F (-9°C).

*See Photo on Page 10.

Salt Water Floats

MESS
METER: 1

NO ADULT
SUPERVISION
REQUIRED

PREP TIME: 15 MINUTES
EXPERIMENT DURATION: 5 MINUTES

Supplies Needed

- ☐ 2 clear glasses
- ☐ 1½ cups (360 ml) warm water, divided
- ☐ ½ cup (120 g) salt
- ☐ Spoon
- ☐ 2 eggs
- ☐ Collection of items, such as pens, small balls, toys, rubber bands and paper clips

Science Question:
Do objects float better in salt water?

Most objects are denser (heavier) than water, so they sink. But when you add salt to the water, it changes how dense the water is, allowing some objects to float. In this experiment we will change the density of water and float objects.

The Experiment

Into one glass, pour ¾ cup (180 ml) of the warm water and set it aside. This will be your control sample.

Into the other glass, pour the remaining ¾ cup (180 ml) warm water. Slowly pour in the salt. Using the spoon, stir it up until it has dissolved. Place 1 egg into each glass. Compare how easily they float between the two glasses of water. Test again with the other items you collected.

The Outcome

The egg in the glass with salt water floats.

Why It Worked

Objects float more easily in salt water. When you added salt to the water, you increased its density, making it easier for some objects to float.

Variation

- Make an egg float in the middle of a glass of water! Fill a glass halfway with water. Add ⅓ cup (75 g) salt and a few drops of liquid food coloring. Stir to dissolve the salt. Slowly add water to fill the glass to right below the brim. Try to not disturb the colored water as you pour the fresh water in. Drop the egg into the water. The egg should drop through the tap water but be suspended above the colorful salt solution.

Invisible Ink

MESS
METER: 1

ADULT
SUPERVISION
REQUIRED

SAFETY
PRECAUTIONS

PREP TIME: 5 MINUTES, PLUS DRYING TIME
EXPERIMENT DURATION: 3 TO 4 MINUTES

Supplies Needed

- ☐ ¼ cup (60 ml) lemon juice
- ☐ Small bowl
- ☐ Cotton swab
- ☐ White construction paper
- ☐ Hair dryer or incandescent light bulb

Science Question:
What happens to lemon juice when it is exposed to heat?

With science we are going to create invisible ink and a super secret way to read the message.

The Experiment

Pour the lemon juice into the bowl. Dip one end of the cotton swab into the lemon juice. Using the swab, write a secret message on the paper. Let the paper dry fully, then hold it a few inches (5 to 10 cm) away from a heat source, such as hair dryer on low or a light bulb.

The Outcome

Your message will appear!

Why It Worked

Heat causes the citric acid in lemon juice to decompose, freeing the carbon. When the carbon touches the air, it turns brown; this is called "oxidation." The magic of oxidation allows someone to read your message!

Variation

- Compare "secret ink" solutions. Try the experiment with other fruits, or a different liquid like vinegar, milk or apple juice. Is your message more or less clear than the one with the lemon juice?

Safety First!

Light bulbs can get hot fast. Make sure you don't touch it.

Did You Know?

The same process of oxidization we see here is what causes apples to turn brown or when something left outside gets rusty, but in those cases no heat is needed.

Solid Water

MESS
METER: 2

NO ADULT
SUPERVISION
REQUIRED

PREP TIME: 5 MINUTES
EXPERIMENT DURATION: 5 MINUTES

Supplies Needed

☐ Scissors
☐ Disposable diaper
☐ Disposable cup
☐ ¼ to ⅓ cup (60 to 75 ml) water

Science Question:
How does a diaper hold liquid?

Diapers have a lot of different parts to them that help absorb liquid. We are going to dissect a diaper to see how they work.

The Experiment

Using the scissors, cut open the diaper. Separate the cotton to find sandy particles. These are silica grains. Dump as many grains as you can from the diaper into the cup. Add the water to the cup. Wait a second, and then turn your cup upside down.

The Outcome

The liquid will solidify, so it won't pour out of the cup.

Why It Worked

When you turned the cup upside down, the water did not dump out as you may have expected. The sand particles of silica absorbed the water, making a gel. When you turn the cup upside down, the gel stays in the cup. It's solid! That's how the diaper keeps the baby dry!

Tip

Avoid touching and playing with the silica water gel. It can irritate skin.

Did You Know?

The National Geographic Society says that the average baby uses 3,796 diapers before he or she is potty trained. That is a LOT of diapers!

Slime

MESS
METER: 5

ADULT
SUPERVISION
REQUIRED

SAFETY
PRECAUTIONS

PREP TIME: 5 MINUTES
EXPERIMENT DURATION: 15 MINUTES

Supplies Needed

☐ Bowl
☐ Liquid starch
☐ White glue
☐ Liquid watercolor paint or food coloring

Science Question:
What's soft like a liquid but holds together like a solid?

In this experiment, you will make an easy slime recipe and explore its colloidal properties.

The Experiment

In the bowl, combine equal parts of starch, glue and paint or food coloring. Use your hands to mix it all up. The key to making good slime is mixing it really, really well.

If after a lot of mixing, the slime hasn't formed well, add a small amount of glue and mix some more. If it's still not forming, add a small amount of the liquid starch.

The Outcome

When you use your hands to combine the ingredients, it forms a solid, stretchy blob.

Why It Worked

Slime is a colloid, or substance that is evenly dispersed through another substance. Your slime has the characteristics of both a solid and a liquid. It moves more slowly than water, yet it is wet, and it slides quickly!

Variation

• What do you think would happen if you added more starch to the mix? How about more glue? How would the slime feel and act differently?

Safety First!

Don't taste the slime!

Did You Know?

Different types of fluids flow at different rates. This is called their viscosity. For instance, ketchup is much more viscous than water. Slime has an interesting property in that its viscosity isn't always the same. It can change, such as if you add stress. This type of fluid is called a non-Newtonian fluid, and other examples are ketchup, yogurt and mud.

Acid and Base Drops

MESS METER: 4   ADULT SUPERVISION REQUIRED   SAFETY PRECAUTIONS

PREP TIME: 1 DAY
EXPERIMENT DURATION: SECONDS TO SEE A REACTION

Supplies Needed

- ☐ Red cabbage, chopped
- ☐ Slow cooker
- ☐ Water
- ☐ Strainer
- ☐ Sturdy white paper towels
- ☐ Safety goggles
- ☐ Substances to test (see variations)

Science Question:
How can you tell if a substance is an acid or a base (alkaline)?

We create a test from cabbage juice to show whether a chemical is an acid or a base. This experiment is smelly and colorful!

The Experiment

This is a stinky experiment—we suggest you do it outside. Place the cabbage leaves in the slow cooker, add water to cover the cabbage, turn it on low and leave it on overnight. The water will turn dark purple.

Strain out the leaves and dip the paper towels into the purple water. Pull them out and hang them to dry. Once dry, the paper towels should be lavender.

Put on your safety goggles. Drip drops of the different substances onto the towels. Watch colors appear on the towel.

The Outcome

If a solution has a high level of acid, it will turn your paper towel bright pink. If a solution is alkaline, it will leave a blue-green stain.

Why It Worked

Red cabbage contains a pigment called flavin, which changes colors when it comes into contact with an acid or a base chemical. Neutral solutions are purple. Acids, such as lemon juice, will turn the flavin red, and bases, such as baking powder, will turn the flavin green or blue. As you drip the solutions, your towel pH test sheet will be covered in a tie-dye of colors.

Variations

- Test apple juice, lemon juice, laundry detergent, soda, baking soda, potato slices, window cleaner, toothpaste, even spit. See what else you can come up with!

Safety First!

Be sure to be outdoors or in a place where the ventilation is good, only mix a drop or two at a time and be sure to avoid inhaling the fumes as the chemicals are mixing.

Underwater Magic Sand

MESS
METER: 3

ADULT
SUPERVISION
REQUIRED

 PREP TIME: 10 MINUTES PLUS
OVERNIGHT DRYING TIME
EXPERIMENT DURATION: 15 MINUTES

Supplies Needed

- ☐ Fine sand
- ☐ Shallow disposable container
- ☐ Fabric protector spray
- ☐ Large glass bowl of water
- ☐ Spoon or other utensils (optional)
- ☐ Plastic container with a lid

Science Question:
Can you make sand waterproof?

Wet sand is heavy and messy! In this experiment, we will coat the sand with a hydrophobic layer to waterproof sand.

The Experiment

In a well-ventilated area, spread the sand out in the disposable container. Spray the sand with a heavy coat of fabric protector spray. Shake the box a few times to make sure it's thoroughly coated. Allow the sand to dry.

Pour the dried sand into the bowl of water. Play with the sand in the water, using spoons to dunk it in and out of the water. Store the sand in a lidded sealed container.

The Outcome

The sand clumps together in the water.

Why It Worked

When you sprayed the sand with the fabric protector, you coated the grains of sand with a hydrophobic layer (or a layer that hates water). This causes the grains of sand to clump to each other in water.

Did You Know?

Hydrophobic sand was discovered near ocean oil spills. People would sprinkle the sand on floating oil, and the sand would mix with the oil and make it heavy enough to sink.

56 The 101 Coolest Simple Science Experiments

Chapter 2

Physics and Making Things Move

You see physics at work all around you: a plane flies, a ball falls, a top spins. It might seem like magic, but it's actually all because of physics.

Holly's pick: The Egg Drop (page 71) has always fascinated me. I love the wild creativity that can be harnessed into something that works . . . or doesn't!

Rachel's pick: Jumping Macaroni (page 76) was by far our family's favorite activity. They made a fountain from a chain of pasta noodles and watched the noodles jump from the pan. Fun!

Jamie's pick: Quicksand (page 90) is one of my favorite things to make because it's super messy and I love how it's a liquid and a solid at the same time!

Balloon Popping

PREP TIME: 10 MINUTES
EXPERIMENT DURATION: 10 MINUTES

Supplies Needed

☐ Balloons
☐ 100 thumbtacks

Science Question:
If one pin pops a balloon, what do 100 pins do?

Typically laying down or stepping on a single nail will pierce you, much like a pin will pop a balloon. But people can lie down on a whole bed full of thousands of nails with no cuts or even scrapes. How?

The Experiment

Blow up a balloon. Place one thumbtack on a table, with the pointy side up. Press the balloon into the tack and see how easily the balloon pops!

Blow up a second balloon. Now place all of the thumbtacks, pointy sides up on the table, close together. What do you think will happen when the balloon comes into contact with a bunch of tacks at once? Give it a try! Press really hard, pushing the balloon into the bed of tacks.

The Outcome

The one tack popped the balloon, but 100 tacks together didn't.

Why It Worked

One tack easily pops the balloon because as you push the balloon down, the tack is pressed into a very small area of the balloon. The balloon pops. However, 100 tacks distribute the pressure along the wall of the balloon, so the force in one area is diffused or lessened, and the balloon won't pop.

Variation

• Press the palm of your hand gently into a single tack. It hurt, right? Try the same thing with the grouping of tacks.
Try the experiment again, only this time spread the tacks out. Is it as effective with the pointy tips farther apart from each other?

Tips

If you're having a hard time keeping your tacks upright for these experiments, consider pressing them through a piece of paper and then putting the paper-filled sheet of tacks upright.

Make sure that you blow both balloons up until they are very full with air.

Did You Know?

The first pushpins were made by hand in 1900. They cost about the same price as the ones you would purchase at an office supply store today.

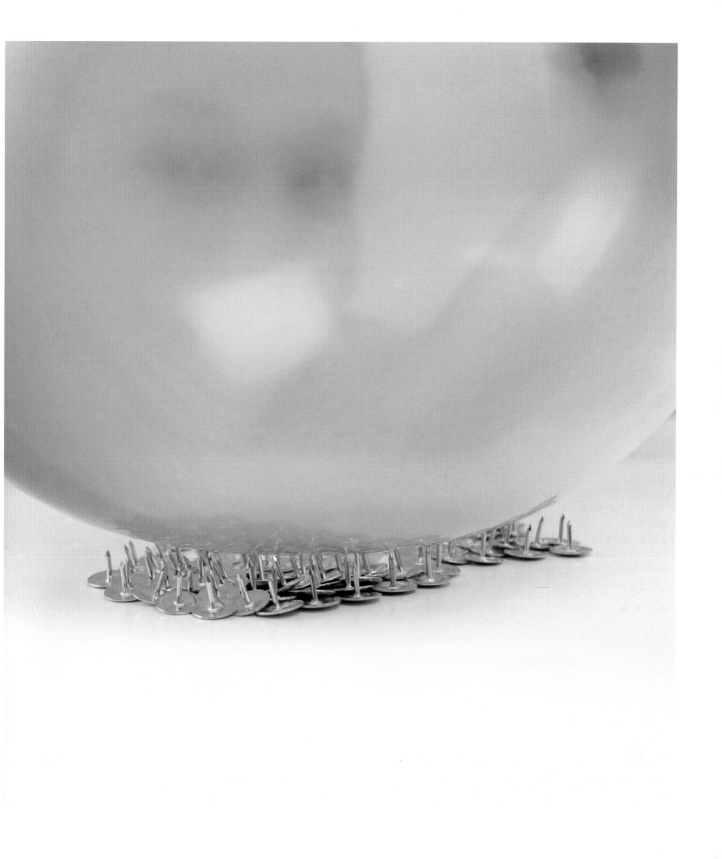

Airplane Launcher

MESS
METER: 0

ADULT
SUPERVISION
REQUIRED

SAFETY
PRECAUTIONS

PREP TIME: 10 MINUTES
EXPERIMENT DURATION: 10 MINUTES

Supplies Needed

- ☐ Paper airplane
- ☐ Paper clip
- ☐ Tape
- ☐ Stool with four legs
- ☐ Several large rubber bands

Science Question:
How can you make a paper airplane fly farther?

In this experiment we will test a way to make a paper airplane fly farther with the help of a slingshot!

The Experiment

First, test your airplane to see how well it flies. You can mark how far it flew.

Next, straighten the paper clip out to form a hook. Tape the paper clip "hook" to the nose of the plane.

Flip your stool upside down so the legs are pointing up. Stretch one of the rubber bands between two of the chair's legs. If necessary, connect several of the rubber bands together to form a longer rubber band chain. Hook the paper clip (attached to the paper airplane) over the rubber band, pull the plane back and let it soar!

Did You Know?

Airplane carrier ships have a similar catapulting device, like a slingshot, that they use to launch planes into flight.

Safety First!

Don't ever aim a slingshot at another person. You can injure someone.

The Outcome

When you used the rubber band launcher, your airplane flew farther.

Why It Worked

By pulling back the rubber band you created resistance and potential energy. As you let go of the band it spent that energy as it returned to its original shape. The airplane was launched into the air.

Did you find that thicker rubber bands worked better? They should—the tighter the bands, the greater the force exerted, the farther your plane will fly.

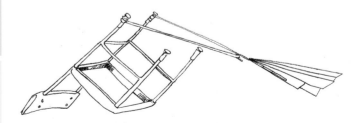

Catapults for Distance

MESS
METER: 0

NO ADULT
SUPERVISION
REQUIRED

SAFETY
PRECAUTIONS

PREP TIME: 15 MINUTES
EXPERIMENT DURATION: 15 MINUTES

Supplies Needed

- ☐ 7 craft sticks
- ☐ 4 rubber bands
- ☐ Tacky glue or hot glue
- ☐ Milk jug cap
- ☐ Small objects to launch
- ☐ Measuring tape

Science Question:
How does a catapult work?

Who wants to launch stuff across the room? A great tool to use is a catapult. In this experiment, you'll make a simple catapult.

The Experiment

Stack 5 craft sticks together and wind a rubber band around each end. Grab the remaining 2 sticks and wrap a rubber band around only one end.

Separate the 2 craft sticks, keeping the banded end intact. Place the stack of 5 craft sticks between the "V" of the 2 craft sticks. Next, wrap a rubber band around all of the craft sticks to hold the catapult together. Glue a milk cap on one end of the stick as a launching platform.

Place your projectile in the milk cap, push down on the top craft stick and release it to launch the item from the milk cap.

The Outcome

When you released the top craft stick, the small toy should have launched!

Why It Worked

When the sticks of the catapult are pulled back, they collect or store up potential energy. When you let go of the top stick, this releases that energy quickly with force. Force causes acceleration, and your object flies.

Variation

- You can use a disposable plastic spoon to make the easiest catapult ever! Put a mini marshmallow on the end of the spoon. Pull the spoon back toward you, let go, and watch the marshmallow soar.

Try This!

How far did your projectile go? Try your catapult again. This time pick a heavier item. Do you think a heavier object will go farther or land closer than your previous launch? Measure and compare how far each object travels.

Safety First!

Don't ever aim a catapult at another person. You can injure someone.

Balloon-Powered Car

MESS METER: 0

NO ADULT SUPERVISION REQUIRED

PREP TIME: 15 MINUTES
EXPERIMENT DURATION: 15 MINUTES

Supplies Needed

☐ LEGO bricks
☐ Balloons
☐ Small tape measure

Science Question:
How does propulsion work?

Rockets lift off with a principle called propulsion (or thrust). In this experiment, we will explore propulsion making our own "jet" from a balloon to power a LEGO car!

The Experiment

Build a car out of LEGO bricks, but leave an opening in the back of your car for your balloon jet. Give your car a little test drive to see how fast and how far it can go.

Blow up the balloon and insert it into the hole at the back of your toy car, so that the bottom of the balloon is facing the rear of the car. Put the car down, let go of the balloon and watch it go! Check the distance with the tape measure.

The Outcome

The car went farther when it was propelled by the balloon.

Why It Worked

When you let go of the balloon, air rushed out of it, causing the car to move in the opposite direction. It is propulsion. Rockets work in a similar way. Exhaust gas comes out of the rocket's engine so fast that it propels the rocket up.

Variation

• Try racing your car on different surfaces. Does it go faster or slower on a rug? On pavement? On a hill?

Try This!

Try combining six eight-stud LEGO bricks (2x4s) in different ways. How many different ways can you combine them? The folks at LEGO calculated this math problem and discovered the exact number of combinations is 915,103,765!

Did You Know?

On average, every single person on Earth owns 86 LEGO bricks! Do you have more than your "share"?

CD Hovercraft

PREP TIME: 20 MINUTES
EXPERIMENT DURATION: 10 MINUTES

Supplies Needed

- □ Valve-style cap from a plastic water bottle
- □ Old CD or DVD
- □ Modeling clay (or hot glue with adult supervision)
- □ Scotch tape
- □ 9-inch (23-cm) balloon
- □ Stopwatch or timer

Science Question:
What can make things hover or float in the air?

Having no weight can make something float in the air, or having something that exerts enough force against gravity to push an object up will also give the appearance of floating. In this experiment, we will make a hovercraft using an old CD or DVD.

The Experiment

With the valve in the "off" position, secure the water bottle to the center of the CD/DVD with the clay and the tape. Create a good seal to keep air from escaping.

Blow up the balloon all the way and pinch the neck closed. (Don't tie it.) Place the mouth of the balloon over the top of the cap. After the balloon is over the valve, open the valve.

How long do you think your hovercraft will hover? Set your stopwatch or timer!

The Outcome

The disc will hover a short distance above the table.

Why It Worked

The airflow created by the balloon causes a cushion of moving air between the disc and the surface below it. This lifts the CD/DVD and reduces the friction, allowing the disc to hover above the table.

Variation

- Change the size of the balloon. Does a larger "reserve" of air affect your hovercraft's ability to hover?

Tip

Try to open the valve only a little bit; this allows the pressure to come out more slowly. Be sure to start your hovercraft on a smooth surface for best results.

Magnetic Slime

MESS METER: 4

 ADULT SUPERVISION REQUIRED

 SAFETY PRECAUTIONS

PREP TIME: 20 MINUTES
EXPERIMENT DURATION: 15 MINUTES

Supplies Needed

- ☐ 1 cup (235 ml) white glue
- ☐ ½ cup (120 ml) liquid starch
- ☐ Disposable bowl
- ☐ Disposable spoon
- ☐ 3 tablespoons (45 g) iron oxide powder (rust)
- ☐ Face mask
- ☐ Disposable gloves
- ☐ Neodymium (rare Earth) magnets (regular magnets are not strong enough)
- ☐ Airtight jar, for storing your slime

Science Question:
Can slime be magnetic?

Slime is a fun substance to play with. It's both a liquid and a solid at the same time. In this book, we include a way to make slime (page 29) and the ways that slime interacts in different recipes. Now we are going to make slime that's responsive to magnets.

The Experiment

Iron oxide powder and magnetic slime are messy, and they can stain, so do this experiment wearing old clothes, on a table covered with an old tablecloth or even outside. Magnetic slime doesn't stick to hard surfaces, and it's easily washed off hands, but it will penetrate clothes and carpet.

Pour the glue and the liquid starch into a bowl. Using the spoon, stir it up. Once it is mixed but still liquidy, add the iron oxide powder. (Be sure to wear a face mask to avoid inhaling the rust.) Mix in the iron particles. Keep stirring continuously for a few minutes. It will thicken and transform into slime before your eyes!

If you don't want your hands to get messy, wear disposable gloves. Take the slime out of the bowl and squish and squash it together with your hands until it's well mixed. Use the magnets to pull and push the slime all around.

When you're done playing with the magnetic slime, you can store it inside an airtight jar.

The Outcome

The slime will get thicker and respond to the magnet.

Why It Worked

The iron oxide powder is really tiny, tiny pieces of metal. When you add iron oxide powder to your slime, the particles of metal make the slime magnetic, so it's attracted to the magnet, which creates a magnetic field—an invisible force.

Safety First!

Put on a face mask to avoid inhaling iron oxide powder. The iron oxide powder is messy and can stain, so be careful.

Copper Train

MESS
METER: 1

ADULT
SUPERVISION
REQUIRED

SAFETY
PRECAUTIONS

PREP TIME: 10 MINUTES
EXPERIMENT DURATION: 5 MINUTES

Supplies Needed

- ☐ 10 feet (3 m) uncoated copper wire (roughly 20 gauge in thickness)
- ☐ Thick marker, any color
- ☐ 6 to 8 disk-shaped neodymium magnets
- ☐ AAA battery

Science Question:
Can you make a wire move without touching it?

Magnets can push and pull against each other depending on their polarity. Let's use this to make our train go.

The Experiment

Wrap the copper wire tightly around your marker, spooling the wire to make a giant "slinky" snake. Remove the marker.

Separate the magnets from each other into two piles. Hold the magnet piles tightly in different hands (these magnets are STRONG), then move the magnets closer to each other. If the magnets "pull" toward each other, flip one of the magnet stacks over and move your hands together again. You want the magnets to repel each other.

Place the battery in the middle of the two stacks of repelling magnets.

Lay your snake out on a flat surface and put the battery train into the tube. If the battery does not go through, pull it out and flip it around.

The Outcome

Your "train" should move through the "tunnel."

Why It Worked

Remember how the magnets repelled each other on both sides of the battery? This created a magnetic force. Inside the copper wire tube, the force pulls on the magnets, making the magnets and battery move, pulling the "train" along.

Variation

- Lay two coils side by side, on the table, parallel and against each other. Put the train on top of your coils where they meet each other and watch! Your train will whizz by even faster.

Tip

Try to keep the coils consistent and not have gaps or bends in your wire.

Safety First!

Do not put the magnets in your mouth.

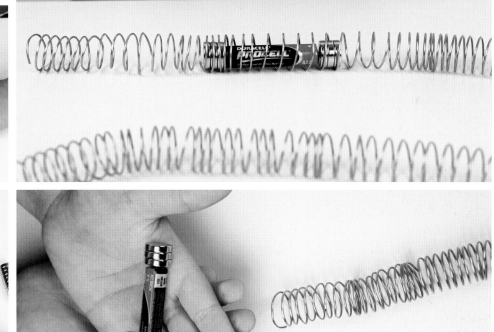

Problem Solving

Is your train buzzing instead of driving? This means you have an open circuit. Straighten your train, or make the coil tighter, and try again.

Is your battery getting hot? This means that you have a short circuit and your positive side is connected directly to the negative. Try flipping one side of the magnets so the forces repel each other, and check that your wires are not crossed.

Egg Drop

PREP TIME: 5 MINUTES
EXPERIMENT DURATION: 15 MINUTES

Supplies Needed

- [ ] 1 dozen eggs
- [ ] Paper towels
- [ ] Supplies to explore, such as plastic straws, Popsicle sticks, cotton, shredded paper, bubble wrap, packing peanuts and cotton towels

Science Question:
What can you do to protect something from a collision?

Car companies ask themselves that question all the time. In this experiment we will test different ways to protect something from impact (fall or collision) using eggs.

The Experiment

Try to create some sort of carrier to protect the egg as it falls, so it won't break. You also want to make something to lessen, or absorb, the impact when the egg hits, such as a soft surface for the egg to fall on to, or you want to find a way to slow down the speed at which the egg falls. Drop the eggs trying different materials to see what works best.

The Outcome

Did you find a way to prevent the egg from breaking?

Why It Worked

As you dropped the egg it gathered momentum and speed. Because eggs are fragile, when the egg collided with the floor, force shattered and splattered the egg. Using something to cushion the fall absorbed the force of the impact before it could shatter the egg.

Variation

- Try to reduce the velocity or speed at which the egg drops. Drop the egg along a draped sheet. Because the egg is falling at a slower speed, the force of the impact will be much less once it hits the ground, and your egg might have a chance at survival. Did it work?

Critical Thinking

Before you begin, predict what supplies will do the best job protecting the egg. Were your predictions correct? Why or why not?

Did You Know?

Much like the cushioning you made for your egg, the bumper and airbags in your car reduce the effects of impact if you get into a car accident.

Electromagnet

MESS
METER: 0

ADULT
SUPERVISION
REQUIRED

SAFETY
PRECAUTIONS

PREP TIME: 15 MINUTES
EXPERIMENT DURATION: 15 MINUTES

Supplies Needed

- ☐ 5 to 10 feet (2 to 3 m) 24- to 30-gauge coated copper wire
- ☐ 4-inch (10-cm) common nail
- ☐ AA battery
- ☐ Rubber band
- ☐ Objects that include iron, such as paper clips

Science Question:
How can you magnetize metal?

A magnet attracts some metals, such as iron and nickel. We can make a magnet using electricity, a wire and a common nail!

The Experiment

Wrap at least 5 feet (2 m) of the wire tightly around the nail, leaving 4 inches (10 cm) unwound on each end. If the wire is coated with enamel, you need to remove that from the coppery ends.

Connect one end of the wire to the negative side (-) of the battery and the other end to the positive side (+). Pull the rubber band over the battery to hold the wires in place. Grab your test objects and touch them to the nail.

The Outcome

Your electromagnet attracted the paper clip.

Why It Worked

When you added energy to the wire, you created an electromagnet. Electromagnets work only when there is electricity running through the wire, creating a magnetic field. Regular magnets do not need an electric current to work. They are always magnetic.

Variation

- Place a bolt on a piece of paper and add some globs of paint. Hold the electromagnet under the paper. Can you make the bolt move through the paint?

Safety First!

When you do this experiment with a larger battery (like a 9-volt), your magnet will be more powerful, but be careful because it can get hot.

Critical Thinking

Why did you have to remove the covered tips from your wire?

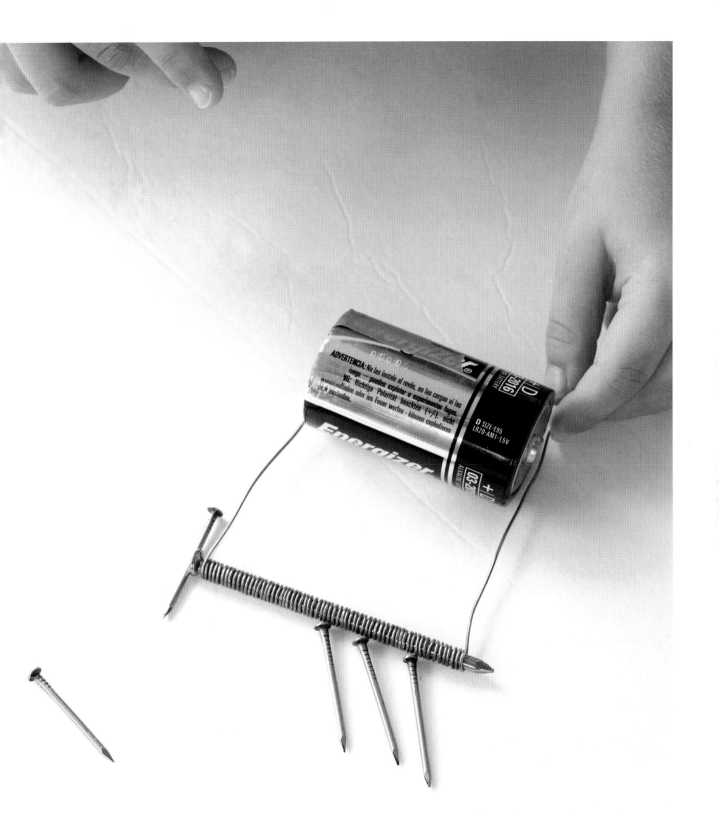

Shiny Pennies

PREP TIME: 2 MINUTES
EXPERIMENT DURATION: OVERNIGHT

Supplies Needed

- ☐ 3 cups
- ☐ 1 lemon
- ☐ Dark soda
- ☐ Water
- ☐ 3 pennies made before 1983

Science Question:
Can you make a penny look new again?

Pennies made before 1983 are made of mostly copper, which turns dull with age. Using the juice of a lemon, or a dark soda, you can make a penny look new again.

The Experiment

Line up the cups. Pour the juice of the lemon into one of your cups, pour soda in another and the fill the last with tap water. Drop a penny into each of cup and let it sit overnight.

In the morning, pull your pennies out of the liquid.

The Outcome

The pennies that were in the soda and the lemon juice will be shiny, but the penny that was in water will still be dull.

Why It Worked

The liquids work as a cleaner, and easily take the gunk and grime off an old penny.

Variation

- What happens if you try to clean a nickel, dime or quarter?

Did You Know?

Pennies used to be made entirely of copper, but they stopped using it when the amount of copper in a penny started to be worth more than the penny itself!

Jumping Macaroni

MESS METER: 1

NO ADULT SUPERVISION REQUIRED

PREP TIME: 10 MINUTES
EXPERIMENT DURATION: 2 MINUTES

Supplies Needed

- ☐ 3 boxes dried tube-shaped pasta noodles
- ☐ Large spool of thin ribbon
- ☐ Bowl

Science Question: Can you defy gravity?

The law of gravity states that what comes up will come down. But sometimes other forces can make it appear that gravity is not working. This is a magic trick where you will make macaroni defy gravity and jump up.

The Experiment

Slide the macaroni onto the ribbon, making a long pasta "snake" in the bowl. You want it to be at least 15 feet (5 m) long, or longer. After you have the string filled with noodles, hold the bowl at about chest height, and toss a few inches (7.5 to 10 cm) of macaroni-covered ribbon out of the bowl.

The Outcome

Your macaroni begins to flow out of the bowl onto the floor, but if you look closely it jumps up several inches out of the bowl before it falls.

Why It Worked

This jumping action is called the Mould Effect. The ribbon and macaroni form a series of hard rods separated by flexible ribbon. It is physics. As one side of the pasta is lifted, the other side pushes down, causing it to "jump." The macaroni appears to defy gravity!

Variation

- Dye your macaroni. Place dried pasta in a glass dish. Pour some rubbing alcohol into the plate. Add a few drops of food coloring. Mix the pasta to make sure it's coated well. Remove the noodles and allow them to dry before use.

Tips

Try videotaping the macaroni jumping; it happens so fast sometimes it is hard to see during the experiment.

The longer the drop, the higher the jump. Try dropping the macaroni over a set of steps.

Did You Know?

Steve Mould recently discovered this effect, which is why this experiment is named after him.

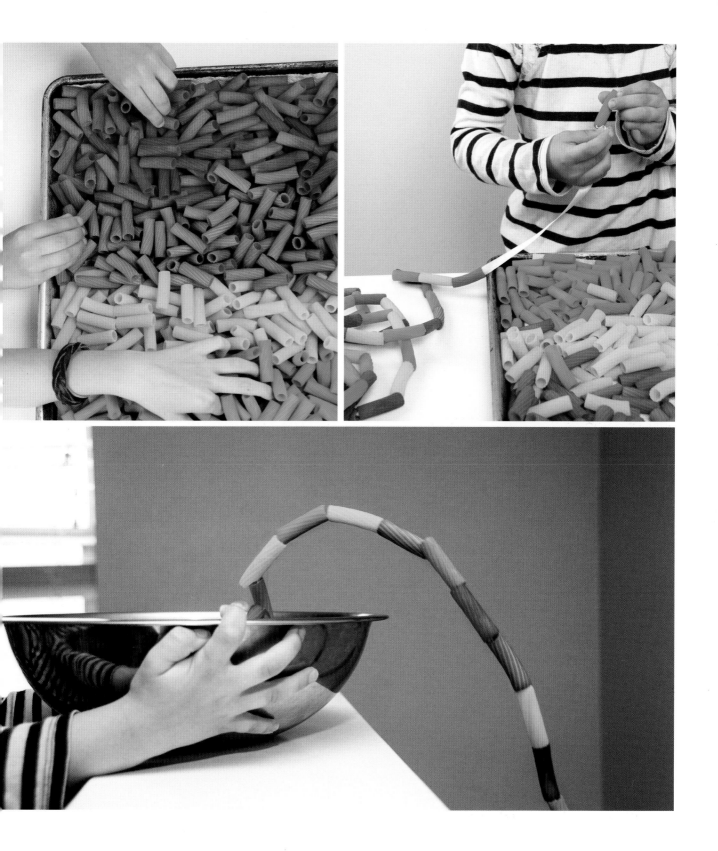

Safety First!

Watch children carefully during this experiment. Iron overdoses in kids can be very dangerous.

Put on a face mask to avoid inhaling the iron oxide powder. The iron oxide powder is messy, and it can stain, so be careful.

Magnetic Mud

MESS
METER: 3

ADULT
SUPERVISION
REQUIRED

SAFETY
PRECAUTIONS

PREP TIME: 5 TO 10 MINUTES
EXPERIMENT DURATION: 10 TO 20 MINUTES

Supplies Needed

- ☐ Face mask
- ☐ ¼ cup (60 ml) vegetable oil
- ☐ Disposable bowl
- ☐ 3 tablespoons (45 g) iron oxide (rust) powder
- ☐ Disposable spoon
- ☐ Clear test tube or tall plastic bottle with a lid
- ☐ Water
- ☐ Glue (optional)
- ☐ Large magnet

Science Question:
How do magnets interact with a semiliquid state of metal?

We will make "ferrofluid," or a liquid magnet, and watch the magnetic mud move in water.

The Experiment

First put on the face mask. Pour the oil into the bowl and add the iron oxide powder 1 tablespoon (15 g) at a time. Stir the powder with the spoon until it is smooth with no clumps. It should have a thick consistency—similar to mud. Once the iron is mixed into the oil, you can remove the face mask.

Fill the test tube or bottle with water. Add the iron-oil mixture to the water 1 teaspoon (5 ml) at a time. Because oil and water do not mix (see page 30), the iron fluid will remain separated from the water. If possible, glue the lid shut to keep the ferrofluid inside.

Use the large magnet on the edge of the test tube or bottle to draw the magnetic mud around the jar.

The Outcome

The magnet will attract and move the ferrofluid.

Why It Worked

Iron responds to magnets, and we made ferrofluid from particles of rust. Ferrofluid looks and acts like a liquid, but because it contains little bits of magnetic-responsive metal, it responds to magnets.

Variation

- Try mixing sugar into your water first to make it denser before dropping your ferrofluid into the tube. Are you able to get your globs of ferrofluid suspended in the water without the help of a magnet?

Did You Know?

Scientists think that the Earth's core is made up of iron and nickel.

Mini Robot

MESS
METER: 1

ADULT
SUPERVISION
REQUIRED

PREP TIME: 30 MINUTES
EXPERIMENT DURATION: 10 MINUTES

Supplies Needed

- ☐ Vibrating toothbrush
- ☐ Long-nose pliers
- ☐ Watch battery (3V)
- ☐ Aluminum foil (if needed)
- ☐ Scissors
- ☐ Double-sided foam tape
- ☐ Decorations (optional)

Science Question:
How can you build a simple robot?

In this experiment, you'll build your own super simple robot! With simple vibrations, it will skitter along the floor.

The Experiment

Break open your toothbrush to reveal the battery, switch and motor inside the handle. Remove those pieces. Test turning on your motor. It should still work after it's been removed from the handle.

Remove the battery and with your pliers cut down the battery section that is attached to your motor and switch, and fold it so that instead of holding a larger battery it is able to fit the watch battery. Fit the watch battery tightly into the slot that you formed. If there is a gap, put a tiny piece of aluminum foil in the gap on one side. Turn on the motor. Does it work? It should!

Cut the head off of your toothbrush. This will be your robot's "legs." With the double-sided foam tape, tape the motor to the head of your brush.

Decorate your toothbrush robot with googly eyes or fuzzy hair from a pom-pom. Give your bot a name. If you are with friends, consider having a bot race and see which one is faster.

The Outcome

Your robot should vibrate and skitter along the floor!

Why It Worked

The vibration of the motor causes the robot to move.

Variation

- Instead of a toothbrush head, try making legs from thin wire. Does this move faster or slower than the robot made with toothbrush bristle legs?

Did You Know?

Robots aren't new! The first robot, made by the ancient Greeks, was a steam-powered pigeon.

Paper Bag Bang

MESS
METER: 5

ADULT
SUPERVISION
REQUIRED

PREP TIME: 2 MINUTES
EXPERIMENT DURATION: 2 MINUTES

Supplies Needed

- ☐ Spoon
- ☐ Cornstarch
- ☐ Paper bag, such as a brown lunch bag

Science Question:
Why does popping a balloon make such a loud sound?

Balloons are fun. But pop one, and the noise can make you jump! In this experiment, you'll discover why a popped balloon is so loud, using a paper bag!

The Experiment

Put a spoonful of cornstarch into the paper bag and then blow up the paper bag with air as if it were a balloon. Twist the bag shut, and shake it a little bit to spread the cornstarch around the bag.

Next, clap the bag hard with your hands to pop it!

The Outcome

The bag will make a loud "thunder" noise when it is clapped.

Why It Worked

The air inside the bag is pressing against the walls of the bag. This pressurized air is keeping the bag inflated. When you whacked the bag and it popped, the pressurized air comes out of the bag in a powerful wave. You can see the wave of air leave the bag with the cornstarch. You heard that wave of air as a loud POP!

Variation

- Test different sizes of bags. Try with a couple of zipper-lock baggies. Different sizes of bags make different noises.

Did You Know?

A paper bag decomposes in about a month, but it can take a plastic bag half a decade to break down.

Paper Bridges

MESS
METER: 1

NO ADULT
SUPERVISION
REQUIRED

PREP TIME: 2 MINUTES
EXPERIMENT DURATION: 15 MINUTES

Supplies Needed

☐ 3 pieces of construction paper
☐ 2 plastic or paper cups
☐ Pennies
☐ Scissors
☐ Tape

Science Question:
What is the strongest type of bridge?

Think about some of the bridges you've seen. In this experiment, you will build a bridge and test it with weight to see if it holds up.

The Experiment

Bridge #1: Fold a piece of paper in half lengthwise. Place two cups upside down on a table about 3 inches (7.5 cm) apart. Put your folded paper on top of the cups, so that the paper "bridges" the gap between the two cups. Place pennies onto your bridge until it collapses. How many pennies did it hold?

Bridge #2: Cut a second piece of construction paper in half lengthwise. Fold each strip on each side to make a U shape. Tape the two U-shaped strips together to form a box. Place the paper on top of the cups. How many pennies do you think this bridge can hold before it will collapse?

Bridge #3: With your final piece of paper, fold it like an accordion. Balance the folded paper over the two cups and place your pennies onto the bridge. How many pennies could this bridge hold?

The Outcome

The first "sling" bridge was not very stable and could not hold many coins. The second "box" bridge bowed in the center, and it was able to hold more pennies. The third "folded" bridge was probably your best bridge. It probably held a lot of pennies.

Why It Worked

In the third bridge, the weight was more spread out along the ridges of the paper, making this bridge the strongest.

Variation

• Try this experiment with longer and shorter pieces of paper. How great of a span can you make?

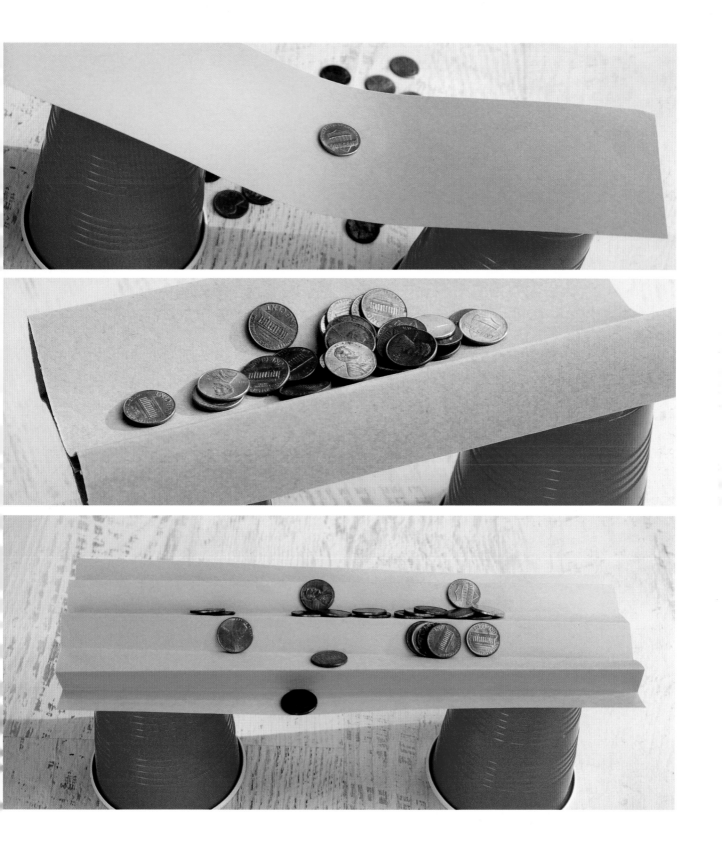

Paper Roller Coaster

PREP TIME: 1 TO 2 HOURS
EXPERIMENT DURATION: SECONDS

Supplies Needed

- ☐ Printer paper, both legal size and letter (regular) size or old magazines
- ☐ Tape
- ☐ Marble

Science Question:
How does a roller coaster stay on the track as it moves?

To learn how roller coasters keep their cargo on the track, you get to explore inertia (which means that something in motion will continue to stay in motion until something stops it), force and energy. To do this, we'll use paper and a marble. Before you drop the marble, there's the potential for a burst of energy. Once you have dropped the marble, it will continue in that state of motion (falling) until something redirects it. Your mission is to control the energy in the marble so that it stays on a track and falls into the pan at the end of the run.

The Experiment

Roll up a piece of paper to make a tube about 1 inch (2.5 cm) in diameter. Secure the tube with tape. Make six similarly sized tubes. Tape them together to make a roller coaster.

Once your roller coaster is ready, drop the marble onto the track and watch it ride the coaster.

The Outcome

Your marble stayed on the track.

Did You Know?

August 16th is National Roller Coaster Day in the United States.

Why It Worked

How does the marble stay on the paper track? Similar to why you don't fall out of loops on a roller coaster: inertia keeps the marble on the track. Inertia is the force that presses your body to the outside of the loop as the roller coaster spins around. Although gravity is pulling you toward the Earth, at the very top the acceleration force is stronger than gravity and is pulling upward, thus counteracting gravity.

Variation

- If you don't want to cut and tape the paper, consider using a ladder and tubing from the hardware store. Using scissors, cut the tubes in half to create a crescent of tubing. You can secure this tubing to the ladder with zip-ties and tape.

Pencil Arrows

MESS
METER: 3

NO ADULT
SUPERVISION
REQUIRED

PREP TIME: 5 MINUTES
EXPERIMENT DURATION: 10 MINUTES

Supplies Needed

- ☐ Zipper-lock bags
- ☐ Sharpened pencils
- ☐ Water

Science Question:
Can you poke a hole in a bag of water and prevent the water from coming out?

Sandwich baggies are made out of a plastic polymer. In this experiment we will see how a polymer reacts to holes being pressed through it.

The Experiment

Fill a zipper-lock bag half full of water. Zip it closed. Hold the bag up and poke the pencil all the way through the bag, so that it goes in one side and comes out the other side. Repeat with more pencils. How much water did you think would spill out? Were your predictions correct?

The Outcome

You can poke lots of pencils all the way through the bag, without (much) water coming out.

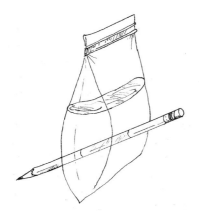

Why It Worked

Sandwich baggies are made of a polymer, or long, flexible chains of molecules. When you poke a pencil into the polymer, it slides between the molecules and the molecules that were spread apart from blowing up the bag then seal themselves around the pencil as they return to their original unstretched position.

What do you think will happen when you pull the pencils out? Hold the baggie over a sink or even outside over someone's head. Pull the pencils out and watch what happens. Because polymers can't seal themselves back together, your bag will spring a leak.

Variation

- Try this experiment with a balloon and skewers. You will need to coat your skewers with dish soap or Vaseline. Push it through the balloon near the tied end through to the other end. It works! Try this again only omit the soap or push the skewer through the middle of the balloons. It failed—interesting.

Popsicle Stick Eruptions

MESS
METER: 1

NO ADULT
SUPERVISION
REQUIRED

PREP TIME: 5 MINUTES
EXPERIMENT DURATION: 5 MINUTES

Supplies Needed
☐ Popsicle sticks

Science Question:
What happens when kinetic energy is released?

If you hold a handful of Popsicle sticks and drop them, you create a crashing and skittering of sticks. You can create a more dramatic effect by weaving the sticks together into particular shapes, and then dropping them. In this experiment, you'll create "explosions" using Popsicle sticks.

The Experiment

To make a simple square stick bomb, place two sticks on the table parallel to each other about the distance of one stick apart. Place two more sticks on top, perpendicular to the first two to make a square. Place another stick down the center. Last, place a stick across the middle so that it goes under the side sticks and over the center stick.

To set your stick bomb off, just drop it so that it lands on its side!

The Outcome

Your "bomb" exploded.

Why It Worked

A "stick bomb" is a pattern of interwoven sticks that are under pressure. When one key stick is removed, the entire structure bursts into pieces. The kinetic energy is released, causing the stick bomb to break apart.

Interwoven sticks can store a surprising amount of potential energy. When you interweave a bunch of sticks, they form a simple "bomb." When one detonates, it sets off a chain reaction. You can make simple handheld bombs or massive, complicated displays from hundreds or even thousands of sticks.

Variations

• Try to increase the force of the explosion by doubling up some of the sticks.

• For older (or at least more patient) kids: Make a Cobra Weave Stick Explosion: Cross two Popsicle sticks into an X shape. Don't make a perfect X; you want two obtuse angles (greater than 90 degrees) and two acute angles (less than 90 degrees). Create a weaving pattern by placing more sticks under the X. If the X were a clock, place the bottom of a new stick, under the end of the X that's at 8 o'clock. Then place the bottom of another new stick under the end that's at 2 o'clock. Continue in this manner until your chain is as long as you'd like. The longer the stick bomb, the longer the explosion. You are creating a chain reaction, which is a process in which putting certain items together promotes the spread of the reaction.

Power Pulleys

MESS METER: 1

NO ADULT SUPERVISION REQUIRED

PREP TIME: 5 MINUTES
EXPERIMENT DURATION: 10 MINUTES

Supplies Needed

- ☐ Broomstick or dowel rod
- ☐ 2 chairs or stair railings
- ☐ Cardboard tubes
- ☐ Tape (optional)
- ☐ Yarn or rope
- ☐ Heavy things to lift

Science Question:
What is a device you can make to help you lift heavy objects?

A pulley is created when rope is draped through one or more wheels, making it easier to lift a heavy object. In this experiment we will make a simple pulley.

The Experiment

Lay the broomstick across the chairs or the railings of some stairs. Slide the cardboard tube onto the stick. This will act as your pulley. If necessary, you can tape your rod in place.

Hang the rope over your paper tube and find something heavy to lift. Attach your object to one end of the rope. Now, gently pull the other end of the rope.

The Outcome

It is easy to lift the heavy object.

Why It Worked

Pulleys make it easier to lift heavy objects. They work because each section of rope splits the weight of the object. You can make it even easier to lift heavy objects by combining multiple pulleys. Add another broomstick and cardboard tube. Is it even easier than before?

Did You Know?

Cranes use pulleys to help them lift massive loads. The largest crane, found in China, can lift 20,000 metric tons.

Quicksand

MESS METER: 4

ADULT SUPERVISION REQUIRED

SAFETY PRECAUTIONS

PREP TIME: 5 MINUTES
EXPERIMENT DURATION: 15 MINUTES

Supplies Needed

- ☐ Spoon
- ☐ 2 cups (260 g) cornstarch
- ☐ 1 cup (235 ml) water
- ☐ Rimmed baking sheet

Science Question:
Can something be both a liquid and a solid at the same time?

In this experiment, you'll make your very own substance that's part liquid and part solid, much like quicksand.

The Experiment

With a spoon, stir the cornstarch and water together on your baking sheet. Once it is lump-free, make a fist and punch the surface of the mixture. Did your hand make a dent? Now try to slide your fingers through the mixture. Were you able to do it? Why?

The Outcome

When you hit the mixture, it felt like a solid. But when you moved your fingers gently, your fingers slid through it, like a liquid.

Safety First!

Discard your quicksand in a trash can because this mixture can clog pipes.

Why It Worked

When you stirred together the cornstarch and water, you created something called oobleck. This substance is a non-Newtonian fluid, which means it changes with pressure or force. The greater the force, the greater the resistance. That is why it resisted the force of your fist but not the gentle movement of your fingers.

Variations

- If you have a whole lot of cornstarch and a baby pool (and a very tolerant parent!), mix 2 parts cornstarch to 1 part water and fill the pool with the oobleck. You can actually walk across it!

- Carefully set the baking sheet on top of a stereo speaker. What do you think will happen when you turn on some music? The mixture "dances" to the beat. You can see the sound waves through the oobleck.

Spinning Egg Inertia

MESS METER: 1

ADULT SUPERVISION REQUIRED

PREP TIME: 5 MINUTES
EXPERIMENT DURATION: 5 MINUTES

Supplies Needed

- ☐ Clear glass three-fourths full of water
- ☐ Thin cutting board
- ☐ Toilet paper roll
- ☐ Raw egg

Science Question:
Why do things keep moving even after nothing is making them?

When you throw a ball, it doesn't drop straight to the ground after you let go of it. The ball keeps going. This is inertia: an object in motion stays in motion until stopped by another force. We will watch inertia in action with an egg!

The Experiment

Put the glass of water on a table. Place the cutting board on top of it. Put the paper tube on the cutting board directly over the glass, and then balance the egg in the top of the tube. Really fast, move the cutting board out of the way—whack it across the room! What happened to the egg?

The Outcome

The egg dropped into the water, like magic! Inertia made it happen!

Why It Worked

The law of inertia says that an object likes to be in the same state. Therefore something moving will keep moving. Something staying still will stay in that place (until someone or something moves it). The inertia of the egg actually held it in the air for a split second, after you whacked the board away, until gravity pulled it into the water.

Variation

- Make a stack of coins at least ten to fifteen coins high; it's best if they are all the same, such as all nickels or all pennies. Stack them and hit the bottom coin quickly with a table knife. The whole stack should just drop down when the lower coin is removed.

Try This!

Find an empty room and spin in a circle as fast as you can until you are dizzy. Then stop quickly. Do you fall a little bit? That is because the fluid in your inner ears is still in motion.

Did You Know?

You can find out whether an egg is rotten without even cracking it open. Fill a bowl with water. If the egg floats, it's rotten! Rotten eggs are filled with a gas called sulfur (it smells terrible), making it float.

Sinking Marshmallows

MESS
METER: 2

NO ADULT
SUPERVISION
REQUIRED

PREP TIME: 2 MINUTES
EXPERIMENT DURATION: UP TO
5 MINUTES

Supplies Needed

- ☐ 4 or more marshmallows
- ☐ Bowl of water
- ☐ Bowl of cooking oil
- ☐ Cornstarch or flour

Science Question:
Why do marshmallows float and how can you make them sink?

Air is lighter than water. Because marshmallows have a lot of tiny, tiny air bubbles in them, they float in water. Get rid of the air in the marshmallows to make them sink.

The Experiment

Drop one regular marshmallow into each bowl. Then, lightly coat your hands with cornstarch and smash two more marshmallows until they are flat like pancakes. Drop the smashed marshmallows into each bowl.

Why It Worked

Smashing the marshmallows removed the air, making the marshmallows dense; this increased their ability to sink. Oil is less dense than water, so that's why the marshmallows sank easier in the oil than in the water.

The Outcome

The regular marshmallows floated and the flattened marshmallows sank. The flattened marshmallows sank easier in the bowl of oil than in the bowl of water.

Variation

- Fill a tall cup half with water and half with oil. Smash a couple of marshmallows. You can get one marshmallow to drop to the bottom of the glass and the other to stay submerged in the oil.

Tip

To keep your ice cream cone from dripping, place a marshmallow in the bottom of the cone, then add the ice cream. The air pockets in the marshmallow will absorb the melted ice cream.

Did You Know?

Ancient Egyptians enjoyed a gooey treat similar to marshmallows as early as 2000 BC. It was considered to be very special, and it was reserved for royalty.

Siphoning Water

MESS
METER: 1

NO ADULT
SUPERVISION
REQUIRED

PREP TIME: 5 MINUTES
EXPERIMENT DURATION: 5 MINUTES

Supplies Needed

☐ 2 containers
☐ Water
☐ Plastic tubing

Science Question:
How does a water tower work?

Have you ever looked at a water tower and wondered why they are often at the top of hills? In this experiment, we will use the power of gravity and the cohesion tension (or stickiness) of water to create a siphon and bring water from one place to another.

The Experiment

Fill one container with water. Place that container higher up, such as on a thick book or an upside-down pot. Place the other container a bit farther away and lower than the first container. Submerge the tubing under the water until it is completely filled with water (no air bubbles). Close one end of the tubing with your thumb and leave the other end in the water. Move the end that you are holding down to the second bowl. Then let go of the hose once it is lower than the water level in the other container.

The Outcome

The water should flow from the raised container to the lower one! As long as there is no "break" in the water, and as long as the second container is at a lower level than the original fluid source, it can flow from one container to another. It's gravity in action.

Did You Know?

Squids and octopodes swim by siphoning power! They suck water in and propel themselves with it.

Why It Worked

First, the drops of water all like to stick together. (This is called cohesion.) The molecules are "chained" together, so they behave like a chain. That's why they appear to defy gravity, moving up and over the edge of the first container and flowing continuously into the other container. Gravity also helps pull the water down.

Variation

• If you don't have plastic tubing, try a smaller project with two bowls and a bendy straw, but it won't be flexible like the tubing.

Tips

If your siphon does not work, check it for air bubbles. The water molecules need to stick to each other for cohesion—it won't work if there are bubbles. Also, the hose must be kept at a lower elevation than the water level.

Have a large fish aquarium you are trying to dump and clean? Make a siphon with your garden hose and you can empty it outside or into a sink with this method.

Submarine Bottle

PREP TIME: 10 MINUTES
EXPERIMENT DURATION: 10 MINUTES

Supplies Needed

- ☐ 12-ounce (355-ml) empty plastic soda bottle
- ☐ Permanent marker
- ☐ Scissors
- ☐ Scotch tape
- ☐ 4 quarters
- ☐ 4 nickels
- ☐ 2 wide rubber bands
- ☐ Flexible drinking straw
- ☐ Modeling clay
- ☐ Large clear bowl filled with water (or use the sink or bathtub)

Science Question:
Why are you able to float in water?

When you're in a pool, if your lungs are filled with air, you can float. But if you whoosh all of that air out of your lungs, you'll start to sink. You can see a similar effect in this experiment, with a submarine bottle.

The Experiment

Place the bottle on its side on a table. Using the marker, on one side of the bottle, make three dots at least 1½ inches (3.8 cm) apart. Use the scissors to cut out a small circle where each dot is.

Tape the four quarters together in one stack and the four nickels together in another. Use one rubber band to secure the stack of quarters just below the hole that is closest to the bottom of the bottle. Use the other rubber band to secure the stack of nickels just below the hole that is closest to the top of the bottle.

Place the short end of the flexible straw into the hole that is closest to the top. Mold the clay all around the top of the bottle and the straw to make a seal so that water can't get in that hole. Place the "submarine" bottle in the bowl of water, with the straw pointing up. Let the submarine fill with water (you can help it by opening up the bottle top). Your sub will then be lying on the bottom of the bowl with the straw sticking out of the water. When your "submarine" is completely under water, blow into the straw.

The Outcome

When you blow air into the bottle, the "submarine" should rise.

Why It Worked

Water is a thousand times denser than air. When you blow air into the bottle, it is lighter than the water, so it rises.

Unbreakable Bubbles

MESS
METER: 3

ADULT
SUPERVISION
REQUIRED

SAFETY
PRECAUTIONS

PREP TIME: 10 MINUTES PLUS OVERNIGHT
EXPERIMENT DURATION: 15 MINUTES

Supplies Needed

- ☐ 3 cups (705 ml) water
- ☐ 1 cup (235 ml) dish detergent, not concentrated
- ☐ ½ cup (120 ml) corn syrup
- ☐ ½ teaspoon rubber cement (optional)
- ☐ Glass jar with lid
- ☐ Spoon
- ☐ Bubble wands

Science Question:
How can you make bubbles last longer?

Bubbles are made of a gas (usually air) that is trapped between layers of soap and water. In this experiment, we'll make (virtually!) unbreakable bubbles.

The Experiment

Combine the water, detergent, corn syrup and rubber cement in the glass jar. Lightly stir with the spoon. Allow the mixture to sit for at least 12 hours before use so the ingredients are fully mixed. Using the spoon, slowly stir the mixture before use.

Use bubble wands to blow bubbles. Time how much longer the bubbles last and how less likely they are to break than ordinary bubbles.

The Outcome

The soap bubbles were harder to pop than ordinary soap bubbles.

Why It Worked

Soap molecules are polarized: one side of the molecule loves water (called hydrophilic) and the other side hates water (call hydrophobic). The soap molecules arrange themselves as a bubble around the trapped air.

Corn syrup and rubber cement increase the surface tension in the soap bubble, making these bubbles harder to pop than ordinary bubbles.

Variations

- With a gloved hand see if you can catch and even pass the bubbles from person to person!

- Bubbles often pop due to evaporation. Blow a bubble into a jar and put the lid on it. In a jar the bubble can last for a longer time.

Safety First!

Discard your bubble mixture in a trash can because this mixture can clog pipes.

Tip

For the best bubbles don't shake the bubble solution.

Zip Line Toys

MESS
METER: 1

NO ADULT
SUPERVISION
REQUIRED

PREP TIME: 5 MINUTES
EXPERIMENT DURATION: 5 MINUTES

Supplies Needed

- ☐ Scissors
- ☐ Straw
- ☐ Dental floss
- ☐ Small toys such as a LEGO figure

Science Question:
How does a zip line work?

Zip lines are fun! They work by the simple principles of gravity and inertia. In this experiment, you'll create your own zip line for a toy to ride!

The Experiment

With scissors, cut your straw into 1-inch (2.5-cm) pieces. Push some floss through each straw "bead" and tie one of your toys to each piece of straw. Next, tie one end of the floss to the back of a chair, hold the line up in the air, above the chair, and put one of the straw beads (and its toy) on your floss. Watch it fall.

The Outcome

When you let go of the straw piece, it slid down the string. That's exactly what you would do on a zip line.

Did You Know?

In some parts of China, kids zip line to school! Zip lines are used by students in Maji, China, to cross the Nujiang River.

Why It Worked

Gravity and inertia dictate that an object is pulled toward the ground unless an opposing force is acting upon it to stop that motion. Adding the string just keeps it sliding down the path of the string instead of straight to the ground.

Variations

- Change it up. Instead of holding the line high in the air, try lowering it so that it is closer to the floor. Will the toys fall faster or slower closer to the floor?

- Instead of floss (which is usually thin and coated) try yarn. Yarn has more friction. How will this affect the fall of your toys?

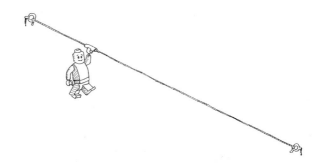

Chapter 3

Exploring the World

The whole world is one big science adventure waiting to be discovered. It is impossible to step out your front door without seeing something that requires further investigation. These learning journeys can be as close as the pebbles underfoot or as far as the stars above.

Holly's pick: I made a Flashlight Solar System (page 122) when I was a kid and loved sneaking it into bed at night so I could look at the "stars" in the dark.

Rachel's pick: Liquid Ice (page 126) is totally fun to watch and create! Kids pour something as water and watch as it instantly freezes. So nifty!

Jamie's pick: I grew a bean in my mouth (page 143) in high school biology class. It's the only time our class was completely quiet!

A58: Aluminum Rocks

MESS
METER: 1

ADULT
SUPERVISION
REQUIRED

PREP TIME: 10 MINUTES
EXPERIMENT DURATION: 10 MINUTES

Supplies Needed

- ☐ 3 or 4 pieces of aluminum foil, about 12 x 12 inch (30 x 30 cm)
- ☐ Safety goggles
- ☐ Hammer
- ☐ Magnifying glass
- ☐ Crayon or pencil
- ☐ Paper

Science Question:
How are rocks created?

Rocks are created in different ways. Some rocks are created by extreme heat and pressure beneath the Earth's surface. In this experiment, we'll create fake rocks using aluminum foil.

The Experiment

Using your hands, wad each piece of foil into a ball.

Squash one ball with your hands or by pressing it into a table. How small or flat can you make the ball? Try again with another ball. Can you make it even smaller? This time, put on the safety goggles and pound the foil ball with the hammer. Hit your foil with the hammer until it's smaller than your first ball.

Make a third foil ball, squash it and whack it like you did with the last one. But this time, pound the foil as hard as you can to smash it as close to completely flat as you can. Some pieces might break off.

You now have three rocks: one big, one medium and one flat. Compare them to any real rocks you have seen.

The Outcome

You just made different types of rocks! Your bigger foil rock is a lot like the surface of clay or mudstone. Take a peak at your ball with the magnifying glass. Clay is made of particles that all face different directions, just like surfaces in your ball of foil.

Your medium-size "rock" is a lot like slate. It is made from clay that has been under so much pressure that it has turned into rock. The particles in it are mostly lined up, facing the same direction.

The thinnest rock is most similar to a type of rock called schist. Did you make any pieces break off with your vigorous pounding? That is called shearing. This rock is more fragile and dense.

Variation

- Go on a rock hunt and see how many different types of rocks you can find. Bring a crayon and put a piece of paper over your rock and make a rock rubbing to remember your specimen.

Did You Know?
Diamonds are the hardest rocks on Earth.

Spinning Marbles

MESS
METER: 1

ADULT
SUPERVISION
REQUIRED

SAFETY
PRECAUTIONS

PREP TIME: 20 MINUTES
EXPERIMENT DURATION: 5 MINUTES

Supplies Needed
☐ Hot glue gun
☐ 4 to 11 marbles

Science Question:
Can you fight gravity?
Gravity makes things fall. To counteract it, we need motion.

The Experiment
Using the hot glue, glue three of the marbles together into a triangle shape. Glue a fourth marble to the center of the triangle, making a pyramid of sorts.

Put your pile of marbles on a flat surface, balance it on one of its ends and spin the marbles.

Gravity usually makes things fall. Try balancing the marbles in an "upside-down pyramid" without spinning it; you can't.

Why It Worked
In order for the pile of marbles to stay upright on the table you need to counteract gravity. As you spun the marbles, you made an axis for the marbles to move around. The momentum of the spin kept the top upright. If there were no friction and the top were perfectly balanced, it would keep spinning for a very long time, indefinitely, much like our planet Earth.

The Outcome
Your marble pyramid should have kept spinning for a while but could not balance by itself.

Safety First!
Using a glue gun is an acquired skill. Aduts can complete this part for younger participants.

Tip
Go big! Add another layer of marbles to your top. Make it eleven marbles big!

Try This!
Have a spinning top contest. See which spinning marbles will spin the longest. You can even have a "battle" and try to spin the marbles into each other. See if the force of your marble pile will interrupt or change the axis of the other spinning marbles' path.

Atom Models

NO ADULT SUPERVISION REQUIRED

PREP TIME: 10 MINUTES
EXPERIMENT DURATION: 10 MINUTES

Supplies Needed

- ☐ Craft pom-poms in multiple colors
- ☐ Craft wire
- ☐ Glue dots

Science Question:
What do atoms look like?

Everything in the world is made of lots and lots of tiny "building blocks" called atoms. We can only see them with a powerful microscope. We will make models of atoms, so you can imagine what they look like.

The Experiment

Atoms are a combination of protons, neutrons and electrons. In our model, each of the pom-pom colors will represent a different part of the atom. Create a nucleus by gluing the proton and neutron pom-poms together into a ball. The wires represent the paths that the electrons take around the nucleus. Cut or bend wires to make the outer rings of electrons. Look at the images of different common molecules and see if you can re-create them. If you have access to a computer, look up other atom molecules to re-create.

The Outcome

Everything in our Earth is made of a combination of these elements. If you could see down to the molecular level of something, you would find these elements in atoms and know what the thing was made of.

Variation

- Instead of pom-poms, you could do this with different colored marshmallows.

Did You Know?

An adult male has around 7,000,000,000,000,000, 000,000,000,000 atoms in his body—that's twenty-seven zeroes!

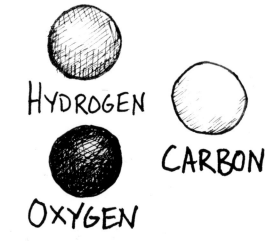

HYDROGEN

CARBON

OXYGEN

Bean Growing Maze

NO ADULT
SUPERVISION
REQUIRED

PREP TIME: 20 MINUTES
EXPERIMENT DURATION: 3 TO 4 DAYS

Supplies Needed

- ☐ Shoebox
- ☐ Scissors
- ☐ Cardboard
- ☐ Tape
- ☐ Small fast-growing plant, such as a bean plant

Science Question:
Do plants grow toward light?

A plant needs and responds to sunlight. We will see this in action with a plant maze.

The Experiment

Turn the box on its side and cut a hole about 2 inches (5 cm) square on one end of the shoebox. This is the "top" of your box. Cut two pieces of cardboard that are half the width of the box and the same height as the box.

Tape one cut cardboard piece on each side of the box, parallel to the "floor" of the box. Water the plant and put it in the bottom of the shoebox. Put the lid on your box, tape it shut and place it in a sunny window.

The Outcome

After a couple of days open the box. Your plant will have bends and twists in it as it moved in the direction of the light coming from the hole.

Why It Worked

A plant moves and grows toward the sun; this is called phototropism.

Variation

- After a few days, take the plant out of the box. Watch and see how long it takes for the plant to straighten out.

Crystal Candy

MESS
METER: 1

ADULT
SUPERVISION
REQUIRED

SAFETY
PRECAUTIONS

PREP TIME: 1 HOUR
EXPERIMENT DURATION: 1 WEEK

Supplies Needed

- ☐ ¾ cup (180 ml) water
- ☐ Pot
- ☐ 2 cups (400 g) white sugar
- ☐ Wooden mixing spoon
- ☐ Potholders
- ☐ 1 clean glass jar or cup
- ☐ Wooden skewer
- ☐ 2 clothespins
- ☐ Paper towels

Science Question:
Can you grow your own candy?

Rock candy is crystallized sugar, and you can "grow" it from a sugar-water solution. In this experiment, you'll "grow" your own rock candy, which is then perfectly safe to eat.

The Experiment

Add the water to the pot and bring it to a rolling boil on the stove (an adult will do this). Turn the heat to low and add the sugar to the water. Stir with a wooden spoon until all the sugar has dissolved. Then turn the heat back up until it is boiling again, and then turn off the heat. Allow the solution to cool for 5 to 10 minutes. Using potholders, pour the sugar water into the jar. (Be careful! Sugar water can burn.)

Clip your skewer with the clothespins, and lay them across the mouth of the jar, suspending the stick in the sugar water. You don't want the skewer to touch the bottom.

Loosely cover the jar with paper towels. Set the jar aside. Watch your crystal candy grow over the next week.

Try This!

Instead of dangling the stick in the solution and using a jar, try a bowl and have the stick lay on the bottom. Did that affect the patterns of your crystals?

The Outcome

Sugar crystals stuck to the skewer and grew bigger as time went on.

Why It Worked

Crystals form by attracting other molecules to join them. When you made rock candy, the sugar crystals "grew" into a delicious pattern of candy!

Variation

- Don't heat up the solution this time. Make a batch with cold water. Predict how successful your crystals will grow. Which were bigger? The jar with warmed solution or the cold one?

Safety First!

Be very careful, sugar and hot water can burn.

Bottle Light Refractors

MESS
METER: 1

NO ADULT
SUPERVISION
REQUIRED

PREP TIME: 2 MINUTES
EXPERIMENT DURATION: LESS THAN
1 MINUTE

Supplies Needed

- ☐ Clean, clear narrow jar
- ☐ Water
- ☐ Black or dark-colored marker
- ☐ Small piece of light-colored paper

Science Question:
How do lenses affect the way we see light?

A lens is something that refracts light to form an image. We have lenses in our eyes and some people wear them on their heads in glasses! In this experiment, we will make a lens from a jar of water.

The Experiment

Fill the jar with water and set it aside.

Using the marker, draw a smiley face on the paper. Turn the paper sideways and slide it behind the jar of water, which is acting as your lens. Slowly move your hand holding the paper back away from the jar, while you are looking through the jar at the paper. Watch the face change!

The Outcome

Holding the paper close to the jar will magnify the smile and make it bigger. But when you pull it back away from the jar, the smile should flip into a frown.

Why It Worked

A lens bends the light that comes into it. In some cases, that bend can make something appear bigger. In other cases, like this "lens" of water, it can even switch the direction of what you're seeing.

Variation

- Instead of drawing a smiley face, try an arrow or the letters of your name. You can even watch your hand or an object be transformed behind the jar.

Try This!

Feeling grumpy? Smile anyway! Even if you're in a bad mood, you can lift your spirits by smiling. Also, like yawns, smiles are contagious. Try frowning when looking at someone who is smiling. It's hard to do!

Chip Can Oven

MESS
METER: 2

ADULT
SUPERVISION
REQUIRED

PREP TIME: 15 MINUTES
EXPERIMENT DURATION: 1 HOUR

Supplies Needed

- ☐ Pointy scissors
- ☐ Clean, empty cardboard potato chip can
- ☐ Clear sandwich bag
- ☐ Tape
- ☐ Kabob skewer
- ☐ Marshmallow

Science Question:
What is sunlight?

Sunlight is powerful! Solar thermal energy can be trapped and used as power or as a heat source. In this experiment, we'll build a solar oven out of an empty chip can and roast a marshmallow.

The Experiment

With scissors, cut a rectangle out of the side of the can in one piece; you might be able to use the "nutrition facts" box—it's the right size. Cover the hole with the sandwich baggie and tape it in place.

Next, poke two holes in the middle of both the lid and the bottom of the can. Push the skewer through the hole in the lid, then put the marshmallow on the skewer, place the lid on the can, pass the skewer through the bottom hole in the can.

Place the can in the sunlight.

The Outcome

Your marshmallow will be gooey.

Why It Worked

The solar energy (sunlight) hit the foil inside your can, and when the baggie was over the opening it trapped that heat in the can.

Variation

- To make the solar oven even more effective, you can wrap the can with an insulator. Try cutting open a drink "cozy" and wrapping it around the can. Does the cooker work more quickly?

Tips

Place the can at an angle instead of facing directly up at the sun for best results. You will probably need to prop it up to keep it in position.

If your can is not foil lined, add aluminum foil around the inside of the can.

Critical Thinking

Which marshmallow would cook faster: one placed in a chip can solar oven in January or one in a chip can solar oven in July? Why?

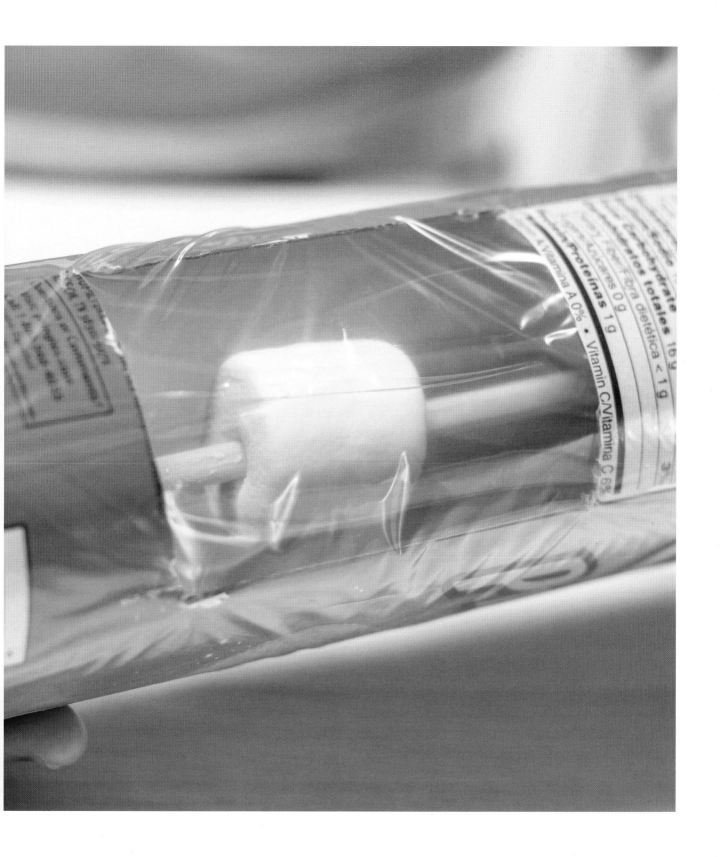

Colorful Cabbage

MESS
METER: 2

NO ADULT
SUPERVISION
REQUIRED

PREP TIME: 3 MINUTES, PLUS
OVERNIGHT TIME TO SIT
EXPERIMENT DURATION: 3 MINUTES

Supplies Needed

- ☐ Table knife
- ☐ 1 large napa cabbage leaf
- ☐ 2 glasses
- ☐ Water
- ☐ Red and green food coloring
- ☐ Dry-erase marker

Science Question:
How do plants drink water?

Using a cabbage leaf and some food coloring, we will experiment with the capillaries inside of plants.

The Experiment

Using the knife, carefully cut a slit up the cabbage leaf, leaving the top third of the cabbage leaf intact.

Fill each glass about halfway with warm water. Add a few drops of red food coloring to one glass and a few drops of green food coloring to the other glass.

Put the glasses of colorful water next to each other. Place a section of the cabbage into each glass. With the marker, mark the sides of the cups so you can see where the water level is. Let the glasses sit overnight. What do you think will happen to the water level in the glass?

The next morning, check out the leaves and notice how much the water levels in the cups decreased.

The Outcome

The water level will be lower the next day and your cabbage leaves will be a lacy spread of bright colors. The colorful lines you see are the capillaries of the plant.

Why It Worked

Inside plants are lots of tiny, long tubes (capillaries) that soak up water and nutrients, bringing them up the leaf through cohesion (see page 94). The water molecules like to stick together until they evaporate. After the water has evaporated from the surface of the leaf, it leaves behind the food coloring.

Variation

- Here's another way to observe capillary action. Fill a bucket with water. Place one end of a thick tube and one end of a thin tube into the water. The water will rise up the tubes at different lengths, rising higher on the thin tube than on the thick one.

Crystal Mountain

MESS
METER: 2

NO ADULT
SUPERVISION
REQUIRED

PREP TIME: 10 MINUTES
EXPERIMENT DURATION: 3 DAYS

Supplies Needed

- ☐ ½ cup (120 ml) hot tap water
- ☐ 1 clean jar with a lid
- ☐ 2½ tablespoons (37 g) alum
- ☐ Spoon

Science Question:
How do crystals form?

You can watch crystals form with this recipe using a kitchen spice called alum. Alum is the ingredient in pickles that keeps them crunchy.

The Experiment

Pour the water into your jar. Slowly add the alum, a little at a time, stirring until it stops dissolving into the water. Put the lid on your jar and let is sit for three days.

The Outcome

The first day you will see a few small crystals have formed in your jar. Each day after that, you will have a bigger mountain of crystals forming in the bottom of your jar!

Why It Worked

The small crystals that form together in a pattern do so because of a process called nucleation. When the alum molecules find each other in the water, other molecules start grabbing on too.

Variation

- Add food coloring to the mix to make a colorful mound of crystals.

Did You Know?

The world's largest crystal was found in Naica, Mexico. It was nearly 40 feet (12 m) long and weighed 55 tons!

Decaying Journal

MESS
METER: 2

ADULT
SUPERVISION
REQUIRED

PREP TIME: 30 MINUTES
EXPERIMENT DURATION: A FEW WEEKS

Supplies Needed

☐ Camera
☐ A fleshy piece of fruit
☐ Notebook
☐ Pencil

Science Question:
How does food decay?

In this experiment, you'll watch a piece of fruit decay and explore what happens in the cycle of life.

The Experiment

Take a photo of your fruit and describe what your fruit looks like in your notebook.

Every day for the next week, examine your fruit. Take a photo and describe how the touch, feel and smell of your fruit are changing. Use your notebook as a journal. Keep an eye out for bugs! If you find any, try to determine what type of bugs they are.

The Outcome

Over time, your fruit looks, smells and feels quite different. It is decaying.

Why It Worked

Decay is when the organic matter of the fruit breaks down into simpler chemical compounds. Decay is caused by bacteria, molds and yeasts. These tiny organisms multiply and grow on dead organic matter, which they eat. They release tiny catalysts called enzymes that break down the matter into very small particles that they absorb.

Variation

• Use multiple pieces of fruit. Predict which will decay fastest.

Tip

If your fruit has a peel or a rind, it is helpful to slice the fruit in half to see the best results.

Did You Know?

One-third of all the food produced in the world goes to waste! The majority of that food ends up in landfills around the world.

Rain Forest in a Bottle

MESS
METER: 2

ADULT
SUPERVISION
REQUIRED

PREP TIME: 30 MINUTES
EXPERIMENT DURATION: WEEKS TO
MONTHS

Supplies Needed

- ☐ Scissors
- ☐ Empty 2-liter soda bottle with cap
- ☐ Handful of small stones or pebbles
- ☐ Activated charcoal (optional)
- ☐ Sphagnum moss (optional)
- ☐ Potting soil
- ☐ 1 or 2 small plants
- ☐ Water
- ☐ Scotch tape or hot glue

Science Question: How does an ecosystem work?

An ecosystem is a self-contained, self-sustaining world, like our planet. It needs living organisms, soil, air and a water system. Earth is one giant ecosystem, but ecosystems can be very small, too. We will make terrariums, or mini-ecosystems, for your countertop.

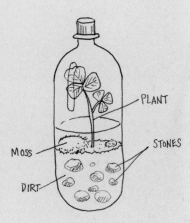

PLANT

MOSS

STONES

DIRT

The Experiment

Cut your soda bottle in half.

Place 1 to 2 inches (2.5 to 5 cm) of small stones in the bottom half of the bottle. Put a thin layer of activated charcoal and/or a layer of sphagnum moss over the stones (we even added a small piece of eggshell). Then add soil to about 1 inch (2.5 cm) from the top of the bottom half of the bottle.

Add your small plants. Water your terrarium so that the soil is moist but not soaked. Place the top of the bottle back onto the bottom bottle portion. Tape it in place with clear tape or secure the seam with hot glue.

The Outcome

Your plants should grow and thrive inside the bottle! The plants create their own ecosystem.

Why It Worked

A plant grows by photosynthesis as it converts sunlight and the nutrients from soil into food. It releases oxygen and tiny molecules of water into the air. This process, transpiration, puts enough moisture into the air to re-water the soil. You should see droplets form on the top of your bottle.

Critical Thinking

Which plant do you think needs more water: a flower or a cactus? Test your theory and make two bottle terrariums.

Tip

Keep your mini-terrarium out of direct sunlight or it will get too hot and your plant may die.

Frosty Salt

MESS
METER: 0

NO ADULT
SUPERVISION
REQUIRED

PREP TIME: 5 MINUTES
EXPERIMENT DURATION: 5 MINUTES

Supplies Needed

- ☐ Large bowl
- ☐ ½ cup (100 g) Epsom salt (magnesium sulfate)
- ☐ ½ cup (120 ml) hot water
- ☐ Few drops dishwashing detergent
- ☐ 1 tablespoon (15 ml) rubbing alcohol
- ☐ Spoon
- ☐ Paintbrushes
- ☐ Very clean clear glass casserole dish

Science Question:
How do crystals form?

Minerals are elements found in nature. They are super small and many of them can form crystals when the molecules of the minerals fit together in repeating patterns. In this experiment you will be able to see crystallization and patterns appear from a mineral solution in mere minutes.

The Experiment

In the bowl, dissolve the Epsom salt in the hot water. If the salt doesn't completely dissolve, microwave the solution for about 30 seconds. Add the dishwashing detergent and rubbing alcohol. The detergent helps make the crystals easy to wipe away when you're done with them and the rubbing alcohol will help speed up the process. Using the spoon, stir the mixture together.

Use the paintbrushes to "paint" your dish with the solution. Crystals will form in a matter of minutes.

The Outcome

The Epsom salt will make snowflake-like crystals on your dish.

Why It Worked

The minerals in Epsom salt form a crystalline structure much like ice crystals do, and this layer of crystal can be applied to a window or any other glass surface.

Variation

- Try this experiment on other smooth surfaces, such as windows or mirrors (get permission first!).

Tip

Make sure your dish is squeaky clean. Try putting your casserole dish in the fridge if it is warm out, before you do the experiment. The frost appears more quickly on cool glass.

Critical Thinking

Dip a finger in butter and make a design on the dish before brushing with the mineral solution. What happened?

Flashlight Solar System

PREP TIME: 5 MINUTES
EXPERIMENT DURATION: 2 TO 15 MINUTES

Supplies Needed

- ☐ Pencil
- ☐ Flashlights, 1 per constellation
- ☐ Black paper
- ☐ Scissors
- ☐ Thick needle
- ☐ Tape

Science Question:
What does the night sky look like?

Constellations are groups of stars that make shapes or images, such as Orion and the Big Dipper. With light pollution and lots of neighbors it is hard to see the stars and constellations. Grab a flashlight, some paper and a dark room, and you can create a small part of the night sky on your ceiling.

The Experiment

With a pencil, trace the front of the flashlight (where the light comes out) onto the black paper. Cut the tracings out to create large circles.

Poke holes into each black circle with the needle in the shapes of common constellations. Tape the constellation circles to the flashlight.

Why It Worked

The light shines through the holes in the black paper, causing it to look like stars in the night sky.

The Outcome

Turn out the lights in the room and close the curtains or blinds. When you turn the flashlight on you should see the constellation patterns.

Did You Know?

According to the International Astronomical Union, there are officially eighty-eight constellations.

Our solar system is called that because our sun is named "Sol." Other star systems have different names.

Cassiopeia

Cannis Major

Orion

Big Dipper

Flying Cups

MESS
METER: 1

ADULT
SUPERVISION
REQUIRED

PREP TIME: 10 MINUTES
EXPERIMENT DURATION: 1 MINUTE

Supplies Needed

☐ Scissors or sharp knife
☐ Dixie cups
☐ Large box fan

Science Question:

Can you use a fan to launch your cups in the air?

Using the air from a fan, we can make cups hover in the air.

The Experiment

Use the scissors or knife to poke a hole in the bottom of your cups, and place a fan on its back. Place your cups upside down on the top part of the fan and turn it on.

The Outcome

The cups hover in midair.

Why It Worked

The air from the fan pushes the cups up, causing them to float.

Variation

• Try this without the hole, with larger cups, napkin or cone-shaped coffee filters.

Did You Know?

Dixie cups got their name because the factory they were made in shared a building with the Dixie Doll Company and the name "Dixie" was already printed on the door!

Floating Needles

MESS
METER: 1

NO ADULT
SUPERVISION
REQUIRED

PREP TIME: 2 MINUTES
EXPERIMENT DURATION: 10 MINUTES

Supplies Needed

- ☐ Clear glass or plastic bowl
- ☐ Water
- ☐ Tissues
- ☐ 2 clean dry needles or paper clips
- ☐ Toothpick

Science Question: How strong is water?

In water the molecules bind tightly to each other and that "bind" creates surface tension. In this experiment, you'll play with surface tension using a few common household items.

The Experiment

Fill the bowl with water.

Separate your tissue into two very thin pieces. Tear off a piece of tissue that's about the size of a large bottle cap. Drop the piece of tissue flat onto the surface of the water. Carefully set a dry needle or paper clip flat onto the tissue, without touching the water or tissue with your fingers.

Use the toothpick to carefully poke the tissue (not the paper clip) until the tissue sinks.

The Outcome

Watch your paper clip float!

Why It Worked

Surface tension is created when the water molecules bind tightly together and form a "skin" on the surface of the water. While it looks like the needle or paper clip is floating, it is actually being held up by the surface tension.

Variations

- Try floating other things, such as pepper or other ground spices. Why do you think they float?

- Put a drop of dish soap in the water. This will bind with the water molecules, breaking the surface tension. The floating clip will fall.

Did You Know?

Some bugs walk on water by taking advantage of surface tension.

Hammered
Leaves

PREP TIME: 10 MINUTES
EXPERIMENT DURATION: 10 MINUTES

Supplies Needed

- ☐ White cotton fabric
- ☐ Variety of leaves
- ☐ Rolling pin
- ☐ Wax paper
- ☐ Hammer

Science Question:
Why are leaves green?

Leaves have lots of color pigments, such as green, yellow and red. But because green is the darkest, in the spring and summer, leaves look green due to the green chlorophyll that they contain. In this experiment, you'll remove the pigment from leaves.

The Experiment

Place the fabric on a hard surface and put a leaf on top. Roll the leaf with the rolling pin to flatten it out, and then cover it with wax paper. Next, hammer the leaf evenly over the entire surface. Try to make sure that the leaf is not shifting on your fabric so you can get the best image from the leaf.

The Outcome

When you pounded the leaves, it released their chlorophyll and other pigments. Some leaf prints will be darker green than others.

Why It Worked

You can tell the health of the leaves by the amount of chlorophyll they release—was your print a dark green or a light green? Or even another color? A plant that is water- and sun-loving, and in a growth cycle, will leave a deeper green print than a leaf that is dying and preparing for winter.

Variation

- Explore the veins in the leaves you find. Instead of hammering them, place the leaves between two sheets of white paper and rub a crayon over them. Identify the parts of the leaf.

Did You Know?

During the life of an average oak tree, the tree will drop 3,600 pounds (1,633 kg) of leaves! That is a lot of raking!

Critical Thinking

Why do you think it is better for a tree to have thousands of little leaves instead of one giant leaf?

Liquid Ice

MESS
METER: 4

ADULT
SUPERVISION
REQUIRED

PREP TIME: 3½ HOURS
EXPERIMENT DURATION: 5 MINUTES

Supplies Needed

- ☐ 16-ounce (500-ml) plastic bottle of soda, at room temperature
- ☐ Plastic or metal bowl

Science Question:
Can something be colder than freezing, but not ice?

You can make magical liquid, liquid that is colder than freezing temperatures, but is still liquid, and watch it turn to ice instantly—super cool!

The Experiment

Put the closed bottle of soda and the bowl into the freezer and go do something fun for three or four hours. Then get the bottle out of the freezer. Be careful not to shake the bottle as you get it out. Pour the drink slowly into the cold bowl and watch what happens!

The Outcome

When you took the soda out of the freezer, it should still have been a liquid, but a super-chilled liquid. As you poured it into the bowl, the liquid was transformed into ice!

Why It Worked

After a couple of hours in the freezer, the soda is colder than freezing. As the beverage hit the cold pan it became solid ice.

Variation

- Instead of pouring the soda into a bowl, open the cap slightly to release the pressure and then lightly bang your bottle. In three seconds, the bottle will fill with ice.

Did You Know?

Coca-Cola alone sells more than 3,500 different soft drinks. If you were to try a different one every day, it would take you nine years to sample them all.

Magnetic Growth

MESS METER: 1

NO ADULT SUPERVISION REQUIRED

PREP TIME: 15 MINUTES
EXPERIMENT DURATION: A FEW WEEKS

Supplies Needed

- ☐ Permanent marker
- ☐ 2 potted plants of the same type and size
- ☐ Several magnets
- ☐ Water
- ☐ Ruler
- ☐ Paper
- ☐ Pencil

Science Question:
Can a magnet make a plant grow faster?

The Earth has a geomagnetic field in its core. This internal magnet in our Earth helps protect us from the sun's solar radiation: it rotates the Earth on its axis around the sun and helps plants grow. In this experiment, you'll compare the growth of two plants—one with magnets and one without.

The Experiment

Using a permanent marker, label one of the pots "with magnet" and the other "without magnet." Place several magnets under one of the pots. Place them in a sunny spot and water them. Measure the plants' growth every few days and record it on the paper.

Why It Worked

A magnet acts similarly to the way Earth's gravity acts on plants' roots, by pulling them toward it. We magnified that effect by adding magnets under the pot.

The Outcome

After a few weeks, the plant with a magnet below it will have grown more than the other plant. Gently pull the plants out of the soil and measure their roots. Are one plant's roots longer than the other?

Did You Know?

Your breakfast cereal probably loves magnets, too. Mash up your cereal and put the dust in a bowl with water. (This only works with iron-fortified cereals.) Hold a strong magnet over the surface of the cereal water.

Hot Ice

MESS
METER: 3

ADULT
SUPERVISION
REQUIRED

SAFETY
PRECAUTIONS

PREP TIME: 1 HOUR
EXPERIMENT DURATION: A FEW HOURS
CHILLING

Supplies Needed

- ☐ 3 cups (705 ml) white vinegar
- ☐ Small pot
- ☐ 3 to 4 tablespoons (45 to 60 g) baking soda
- ☐ Spoon
- ☐ Plastic container with lid

Science Question:
Is ice always cold?

Did you know ice can be hot? In this experiment, you'll find out how different chemicals freeze at different temperatures with two ingredients from your kitchen!

The Experiment

In the sink, pour the vinegar into your pot. Slowly add the baking soda a little at time, stirring with the spoon between additions. Don't pour it in too quickly, or you'll get a messy baking soda volcano!

Put the pot on the stove over high heat. Boil the solution to concentrate it, until a crystal skin starts to form on the surface. This might take an hour or so and your liquid might change colors and become yellow or brown.

After the crystals form on the surface, remove the pot from the heat and carefully pour the solution into the container. Take a look at the liquid. Do you see crystals floating in it? If so, stir a very small amount of water or vinegar into the solution, just sufficient to dissolve the crystals. Put the lid on the container and put it in the refrigerator to chill. Check your pot; there should be some leftover crystals on the edge of the container. Scrape some of these out and put them on a separate plate.

After a couple of hours take your liquid out of the refrigerator. It should be a liquid still. Drop the scrapings from your pot onto the liquid and watch! Now touch the side of your container.

The Outcome

Your "ice" will be warm when it meets with more of the crystals!

Why It Worked

When you combine the vinegar and baking soda, and put it over heat you made a concentrated solution of sodium acetate. Sodium acetate freezes at 140°F (60°C). When you chilled it to below its melting point, it caused the liquid to form crystals, or hot ice.

Safety First!
Parents should use the stove!

Tip
Want to do this experiment again? Simply heat the crystals up past their melting point in order to re-dissolve the sodium acetate and then cool the liquid to create the supersaturated solution.

Moon Craters

MESS
METER: 3

NO ADULT
SUPERVISION
REQUIRED

PREP TIME: 2 MINUTES
EXPERIMENT DURATION: 15 MINUTES

Supplies Needed

- ☐ Large, rimmed cookie sheet
- ☐ Flour
- ☐ Teaspoon
- ☐ Ruler
- ☐ Small toys, such as marbles, bouncy balls and cars

Science Question:
What happens in space when a meteor collides with a planet?

When you look at the moon, there are lots of spots. Many of these spots are craters. Craters were formed by asteroids or comets crashing into the moon, after being drawn to the moon by the moon's gravitational pull. Because the moon lacks an atmosphere or weather, the craters remain well preserved for years, even centuries.

In this experiment, we will simulate crater formation using flour and small toys.

The Experiment

Cover the bottom of the cookie sheet with ½ inch (1.3 cm) of flour. Fill the teaspoon with flour. Using the ruler, measure how wide across the spoon is when it has flour on it.

Drop the spoonful of flour onto the tray and measure the size of the "crater" that is left behind.

Now do the same thing with small toys of different shapes and sizes. Vary the height from which you drop the toys. Does the size of the crater change when you drop the items higher or lower to the baking sheet?

The Outcome

The flour and toys created craters of different depths and sizes, depending on their height and weight.

Why It Worked

As an asteroid or comet from space hits the moon, it creates a depression, or crater. The crater's size and features depend on the mass, velocity and incoming angle of the asteroid or comet.

Variation

- To create different layers of material for the craters to form, instead of just flour, fill the baking sheet with 4 inches (10 cm) of sand, sugar, rice or oatmeal. Then add 1 to 2 inches (2.5 to 5 cm) of flour. With a sifter, sprinkle a thin layer of powdered cocoa on top, just covering the flour. Drop items onto the baking sheet to see how many layers the impact goes through.

Did You Know?

Because the moon is smaller than planet Earth, it has a weaker gravity field. On the moon, you would weigh about one-sixth (16.5 percent) of your weight on Earth.

Egg in a Bottle

MESS
METER: 1

ADULT
SUPERVISION
REQUIRED

SAFETY
PRECAUTIONS

PREP TIME: 5 MINUTES
EXPERIMENT DURATION: 5 MINUTES

Supplies Needed
- ☐ Clean, dry glass bottle with an opening a little smaller than an egg
- ☐ Hard-boiled egg, peeled
- ☐ 4 matches

Science Question:
What are the effects of differences in air pressure?

Air is everywhere and is constantly putting pressure on your body. In this experiment, you will see what happens when we change the air pressure.

The Experiment

Set the bottle on a table and put your peeled egg over the mouth of the bottle. Light a match, move the egg and quickly drop the lit match into the bottle. Do it again with the other matches, each time quickly putting the egg back over the mouth of the bottle. (An adult should light the matches.)

The Outcome

The egg will wiggle on top of the bottle and then be sucked into the bottle!

Safety First!

Never, ever play with matches or use them without an adult present.

Why It Worked

The lit matches heated the air inside the bottle. The hot air expands and takes up more room, and some of the air escaped out of the bottle. That's why you saw your egg wiggle on top of the bottle.

As the matches burn out, the air cools and takes up less room inside the bottle. The result is lower pressure inside the bottle. Wind is when warm air rushes toward the cool air, and normally the air outside the bottle would come rushing in to fill the bottle, but the egg was in the way! That pressure pushed the egg into the bottle.

Variations

- To do the opposite experiment and get the egg out of the bottle, blow a gust of air into it. The egg will come out quickly!

- You can also try this experiment with a water balloon that's about the size of a tennis ball. Does it go in more quickly or slowly than the egg?

Tea Rocket

MESS
METER: 3

ADULT
SUPERVISION
REQUIRED

SAFETY
PRECAUTIONS

 PREP TIME: 2 MINUTES
EXPERIMENT DURATION: LESS THAN
1 MINUTE

Supplies Needed
- ☐ Scissors
- ☐ Tea bags
- ☐ Safety glasses
- ☐ Lighter or matches

Science Question:
What happens when air gets hot really fast?

When hot air rises and colder air forms below, it creates movement in the air.

The Experiment

Important: This experiment should be done on a nonflammable surface, like a plate or a sidewalk.

Cut the stapled end off of the tea bag to make a tube and stand it up on your nonflammable surface. Put on your safety glasses. Have an adult help you use a lighter or match to light the top of the tea bag. Step back and be patient. It will take a few moments for the molecules to heat up.

The Outcome

The tea bag will shoot up into the air and then fall to the ground.

Why It Worked

When the molecules heat up, the tea bag shoots several feet up into the air until all the energy has dissipated from the tea bag. When the fire goes out and the air gets cold again, the bag will fall.

Variations

- Use a spaghetti noodle as a match and try igniting closer to the bottom of the tea bag. Does the tea bag rocket still work?

- Try this experiment with a different material like a coffee filter. Can you still generate lift? How might the material affect its ability to fly?

Safety First!

Never, ever play with matches or lighters or light a match or lighter without a grown-up present. Fires can grow quickly, and they can hurt you and damage things. Be safe!

Did You Know?

Tea is the second most widely consumed beverage in the world after water. Almost 80 percent of U.S. households have tea. It is the only beverage commonly served hot or iced, anytime, anywhere, for any occasion.

Rain
in a Cup

MESS
METER: 3

NO ADULT
SUPERVISION
REQUIRED

PREP TIME: 5 MINUTES
EXPERIMENT DURATION: 10 MINUTES

Supplies Needed

☐ Clear plastic or glass cup
☐ Water
☐ Shaving cream
☐ Food coloring

Science Question: Why does it rain?

The rain that falls from the sky comes from clouds. The water on Earth heats up, turns to vapor, travels up into the atmosphere and forms clouds. The clouds grow, becoming heavier and heavier. Once the clouds reach a critical point, they become too heavy, and the droplets fall in rain back to the Earth. In this experiment, you'll make food coloring "rain" fall from a shaving cream "cloud"!

The Experiment

Fill the cup three-quarters full with cold water. Spray shaving cream on top, covering the water completely with a layer of shaving cream. Add a few drops of food coloring to the top and watch.

The Outcome

The food coloring will rain down through the shaving cream into the water. The food coloring will not disperse right away in the water.

Why It Worked

In this experiment, the shaving cream represents clouds, the water represents air and the food coloring represents precipitation. As the food coloring "precipitation" saturates the shaving cream "cloud," it becomes heavy. When the "cloud" can no longer hold it, the food coloring "rains" down through the water, like rain falls down through the air. The molecules in the cold water move slowly, so it takes longer for the food coloring to spread through the water.

Variation

• Try this experiment with warm and even hot water. Does the temperature of the water affect the outcome?

Did You Know?

The driest place on Earth isn't the desert! It's Antarctica. Even though Antarctica is covered with ice, it only gets about 6½ inches (16 cm) of rain or snow per year. North America gets about 250 inches (6.4 m) of rain each year.

Did You Know?

On other moons and planets, rain is made of sulfuric acid or methane. On a planet 5,000 light-years away, scientists found raindrops made of iron rather than water. Some scientists say it might even rain diamonds on Jupiter!

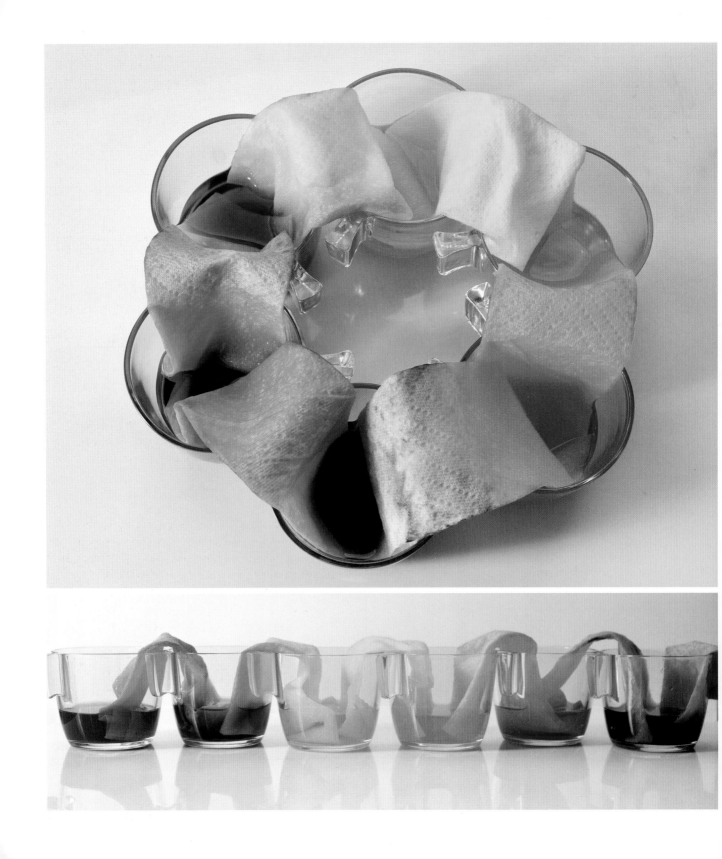

Rainbow Water

MESS
METER: 2

NO ADULT
SUPERVISION
REQUIRED

PREP TIME: 5 MINUTES, PLUS A FEW HOURS OR OVERNIGHT TO SIT
EXPERIMENT DURATION: 15 MINUTES

Supplies Needed
- ☐ Scissors
- ☐ Paper towels
- ☐ 6 clear glasses
- ☐ Water
- ☐ Red, blue and yellow food coloring

Science Question:
How does a paper towel soak up a spill?

Paper towels, like the trees they come from, soak up the water through "capillary action." The plant fibers pull the water up the towel.

The Experiment

Cut the paper towels into six strips that are roughly 4 inches (10 cm) wide. Fold them in half to make 2-inch (5-cm) strips.

Fill three of the glasses almost to the top with water. Add food coloring to each cup (one red, one blue, one yellow). You will probably need ten or so drops of food coloring per cup. Place the glasses in a circle, alternating with the three empty glasses.

Drape the paper towel strips between the glasses so half of each towel is in a colored glass and the other half is in an empty glass.

The Outcome

The water in the filled glasses will climb up the paper towels, through the plant fibers, and drip into the empty glasses. The colors will begin to combine. Red and blue will mix to become purple, yellow and red will make orange, and yellow and blue will make green.

Let the glasses and towels sit in the jars for a few hours or even overnight. The towels and glasses will look like a color wheel!

Why It Worked

The capillaries (tiny, long tubes) in the plant fibers soak up the water, bringing them up the paper towel through cohesion (where the water molecules stick together).

Variation

• See how high you can get water to climb! Try this experiment with a dish of water and a longer length of paper towels, suspended a couple of feet (m) in the air, such as off the edge of a table, and dropped into the dish.

Did You Know?

Paper towels were invented after a batch of bad toilet paper couldn't be sold. Arthur Scott in 1907 repurposed the failed paper into towel-size sheets and viola!—disposable towels.

Expanding Seeds

PREP TIME: 10 MINUTES
EXPERIMENT DURATION: 10 MINUTES

Supplies Needed

- ☐ Various types of seeds, such as wheat berries, flaxseeds, chia seeds and basil seeds
- ☐ Glass cups
- ☐ Measuring cup
- ☐ Water
- ☐ Magnifying glass

Science Question: How do seeds germinate?

For seeds to produce more plants, they have to germinate first. We are going to watch our seeds at the very beginning of the plant growing process.

The Experiment

Place a small amount of each seed in each cup. We used food seeds from our cupboard so we could measure out 4 tablespoons (40 g) of each seed. Then measure the same amount of water and add that to each cup of seeds. Let the seeds set for a few minutes. It might take a couple of minutes and for some seeds it might take a full day, but you should see some changes in the seeds!

The Outcome

As seeds soak up the water they will need for the plant to grow, they become swollen and slimy.

Why It Worked

Look at a dry seeds with a magnifying glass: Can you see a tiny hole? That is the micropyle. The seed absorbs water through that hole, allowing the seed to germinate and begin to grow.

Variations

- Weigh the wet seeds to compare their weights to the dry seeds.

- Ask an adult to use a knife to peel off the outer layer of the seeds to see what's inside! You can easily peel off the testa (the outer covering) to see the embryo (the part that will develop into a plant) and the cotyledons (the first leaves of the plant).

Try This!

Try this experiment again, only use the same seeds and compare their germination rates when you use different beverages, such as milk, orange juice, soft drinks and sports drinks, instead of water. Do you think that the time to germinate will be affected by the type of beverage? Make predictions. Were your predictions correct?

The Life of a Flame

MESS
METER: 2

ADULT
SUPERVISION
REQUIRED

SAFETY
PRECAUTIONS

PREP TIME: 2 MINUTES
EXPERIMENT DURATION: 30 MINUTES

Supplies Needed

☐ Matches
☐ Nonflammable surface
☐ Small dry twigs
☐ Glass cup

Science Question:
How does a fire die?

There is something about watching a fire that is mesmerizing. Fire looks like it is alive. In this experiment, you will record the life span of a fire.

The Experiment

Warning: Have an adult present for this experiment and be sure to pick a safe location: we suggest your driveway.

Watch as your parent lights a match. Put the lit match down on the sidewalk and watch what happens. The fire will go out relatively quickly. Next, light another match and hold it up to one end of the twig. Once the end of the twig is lit, watch it for a minute and then take the cup and cover the twig. What happens?

The Outcome

When the cup covered the twig, the fire went out.

Why It Worked

For a fire to burn, it needs several elements: fuel, oxygen and energy or heat. If you take away even one of these elements, a fire will extinguish or go out. In this experiment, the twigs are the fuel. With no fuel (like the match) the fire went out. Oxygen is in the air that we breathe; when we covered the flame with the cup it took away the oxygen and the fire went out.

Carbon is in all organic materials, or in other words, in things that were at one time living. As the fire burns, it leaves behind the carbon as ash and possibly a piece of charcoal.

Variation

• Do the experiment again, only compare two pieces of paper. Wad one into a ball and fold the other into a very tight square. Which do you think will burn faster? Why?

Safety First!

Never play with matches or lighters without an adult present. Fires can grow quickly, and they can hurt you and damage things. Be safe!

Did You Know?

Lab-created diamonds are made from carbon or ash that is pressed into a diamond stone, called cubic zirconia.

Tornado in a Bottle

MESS METER: 1

NO ADULT SUPERVISION REQUIRED

PREP TIME: 5 MINUTES
EXPERIMENT DURATION: 5 MINUTES

Supplies Needed

- ☐ Washer that is the same size as your bottle's mouth
- ☐ 2 matching tall water bottles
- ☐ Water
- ☐ Glitter
- ☐ Food coloring
- ☐ Duct tape

Science Question:
What does a tornado look like?

A tornado is a rotating column of air extending from a thunderstorm to the ground. We will create a mini tornado from water—in a jar!

The Experiment

Find a washer that is roughly the same size around as the mouth of your bottle. Fill one bottle with water, food coloring and glitter, and place the washer as a "lid" to the bottle. Take your empty bottle and place it over the full bottle. Match up the mouths of the bottle and duct tape them together to create a seal.

Turn your taped-together bottles over. What do you think will happen? Did you expect the water to pour into the bottom bottle? It didn't, right? There is something in the bottom bottle: air. Air pressure is keeping the water from coming down. Now, swirl your bottles.

Did You Know?
Tornados form on every continent except Antarctica.

The Outcome

You created a mini tornado inside the bottle!

Why It Worked

Swirling the joined-together bottles created a vortex (a swirling column of liquid) as the air pressure inside the bottom bottle was displaced, or moved, into the upper bottle.

Variation

- Try this experiment with only one bottle. Fill your bottle with water, glitter, even small objects like a paper clip or pom-pom. Put the cap on tightly and swirl. Watch the tornado form.

Homemade Volcano

MESS METER: 4

ADULT SUPERVISION REQUIRED

PREP TIME: 10 MINUTES
EXPERIMENT DURATION: 2 MINUTES

Supplies Needed
- ☐ 1 tablespoon (15 g) baking soda
- ☐ Empty plastic bottle
- ☐ Funnel
- ☐ 2 cups (470 ml) vinegar

Science Question:
What does it look like when a volcano erupts?

Have you ever seen a volcano erupt on TV or in a movie? They are very violent! Volcanoes are openings in the Earth. When they're active, they can spew ash, gas and magma (liquefied rock) for many miles.

The Experiment
Pour the baking soda into your plastic bottle. Using your funnel, pour the vinegar into the baking soda and watch the eruption!

Why It Worked
It is pretty awesome to discover what happens when vinegar and baking soda mix. They combine inside the bottle and are forced out the small opening similar to how a volcano erupts.

The Outcome
The vinegar expanded and spewed out from the bottle.

Variation
- Add some glitter or food coloring to your vinegar for a sparkly, colorful explosion.

Did You Know?
The biggest known volcano in our solar system is on Mars. Its name is Olympus Mons. It's 373 miles (600 km) wide and 13 miles (21 km) high. If it were a highway, it would take you six hours to drive around!

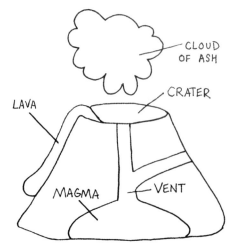

CLOUD OF ASH

CRATER

LAVA

MAGMA

VENT

Grow a Bean in Your Mouth

MESS
METER: 1

ADULT
SUPERVISION
REQUIRED

SAFETY
PRECAUTIONS

PREP TIME: OVERNIGHT
EXPERIMENT DURATION: 30 MINUTES

Supplies Needed

- ☐ Dried bean
- ☐ Cup of water
- ☐ Paper towel
- ☐ Your mouth

Science Question:
How fast can a bean grow?

We are going to use the carbon dioxide and saliva in our mouth to make a bean sprout in 30 minutes.

The Experiment

Take a bean and soak it overnight in a cup of water. Pull your bean out of the water and pat it dry with a paper towel. Place the bean under your tongue for 30 minutes, and do not open your mouth!

The Outcome

When you open your mouth and pull out your bean, it will have sprouted in your mouth right under your tongue!

Why It Worked

When you leave the bean in your mouth, the carbon dioxide creates the perfect environment to sprout your bean.

Variation

- Put your bean in a baggie with a paper towel and tape it to a window. See how long it takes to sprout that way.

Did You Know?

Beans were used in ancient Rome to decide who got the important jobs. Employers would mix a black bean in with a bunch of white beans, and whoever drew the black bean got the job!

Safety First!

Beans shouldn't be consumed in large quantities raw. This experiment should be supervised.

Current Colors

PREP TIME: OVERNIGHT
EXPERIMENT DURATION: 5 MINUTES

Supplies Needed

- ☐ Ice cube tray
- ☐ Water
- ☐ Blue and red food coloring
- ☐ Large clear bowl
- ☐ Glass cup

Science Question:
Can you make a current?

Cold air is denser than warm air, and the same is true with water. In this experiment, we will watch what happens when cold air is introduced to warm air, using water.

The Experiment

Fill the ice cube tray with water and add three or four drops of blue food coloring to each cube. Set that in the freezer to harden. Fill your large bowl with water. Stop a couple of inches (cm) from the top and set it on the counter overnight. You want this bowl of water to reach room temperature.

The next day, fill your glass cup with water and microwave it until it is starting to boil. Add red food coloring until it is a dark red color. Remove the blue cubes from the freezer. Put two or three of the cubes in your bowl of water. Watch for a minute to see what happens to the blue water as it melts from the cube.

Gently pour the hot red water into one side of your bowl (use about the same amount of hot red water as you do cold blue ice).

The Outcome

Your water will become striped. You will see hot red water working itself to the top, warm clear water in the middle and cold blue water working itself to the bottom.

Why It Worked

Hot water takes up more space than cold water does. When the water is boiled, bubbles form: these are gases escaping. This water is lighter. The blue ice cubes are frozen water. When the molecules are cold they become denser and heavier. You can see how the hot water stays at the top of the bowl, because it is lighter, and the blue water sinks to the bottom of the bowl, because it is heavier. As the hot water cools and the cold water warms, they mix and become purple.

Try This!

Fill a balloon with air. Measure the circumference of the balloon. Stick it in the freezer. After an hour, pull it out of the freezer and measure it again. What happened to the air molecules in the balloon?

Weigh Gas

MESS
METER: 1

NO ADULT
SUPERVISION
REQUIRED

PREP TIME: 15 MINUTES
EXPERIMENT DURATION: 2 MINUTES

Supplies Needed

☐ Binder clip
☐ Ruler
☐ Pencil or pen
☐ Heavy book
☐ 2 balloons
☐ Tape
☐ Paper

Science Question:
How can we weigh air?

We are surrounded by gases. In this experiment, we will make a simple scale using office supplies to weigh two common gases, a nitrogen-oxygen blend and carbon dioxide.

The Experiment

Clip the binder clip over the center of your ruler. Push one side of the clip down and leave the other up as a "hanger." Stick your pencil through the slot. Lay the pencil over the edge of a table and put the book over the pencil to hold it in place. Check to make sure the ruler is level.

Blow up one balloon with air (roughly 80 percent nitrogen and 20 percent oxygen) and fill the other with carbon dioxide (use the experiment on page 15). Tape each balloon to opposite ends of the ruler, and mark which is which on a piece of paper. Which do you think will weigh more?

The Outcome

The balloon filled with carbon dioxide will hang lower than the balloon filled with air.

Why It Worked

The denser a gas is, the heavier it is. The balloon that is filled with the heavier carbon dioxide will hang lower than the balloon filled with the lighter air.

Variation

• Now that you've created your very own simple scale, you can use it to measure other things as well! Instead of taping balloons to the ruler, try suspending envelopes with strings and tape one to either end of the ruler. You can compare the weights of different objects by putting them in the envelopes.

Did You Know?

Radon is the heaviest gas. It is more than seven times heavier than the air we breathe.

vinegar

Chapter 4

The Human Body

The human body holds more science secrets than we could learn in a lifetime. Even a simple thing like drinking a glass of water puts thousands of processes in play.

Rachel's pick: It is great to see how important strong bones are with the experiment Bendy Bones (page 173). You can make a bone bend in unbelievable ways.

Holly's pick: After dinner, one of my family's favorite things to do is an impromptu concert with Singing Cups (page 167).

Jamie's pick: Glitter Germs (page 157) is so fun because you can really see how germs spread with something as simple as the touch of a hand!

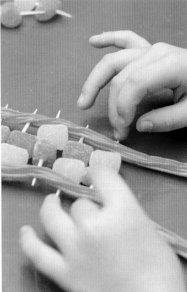

DNA Models

MESS
METER: 2

NO ADULT
SUPERVISION
REQUIRED

PREP TIME: 15 MINUTES
EXPERIMENT DURATION: 5 MINUTES

Supplies Needed

- ☐ At least 40 assorted gummy candies in 4 different colors
- ☐ 20 toothpicks
- ☐ 2 pieces of licorice

Science Question:
What does DNA look like?

DNA is an acronym for deoxyribonucleic acid. These molecules tell the body how to develop and function. But what does DNA look like? We will make a model of a DNA strand using candy.

The Experiment

Divide the candies into piles by color. Then pair up the colors (example: green with red and blue with yellow).

Slide one pair of candies onto the center of each toothpick. Then, holding the licorice pieces, stick one end of the toothpicks into each piece of licorice, like railroad tracks. To make the double helix shape, simply give it a twist!

The Outcome

The licorice represents the "backbone" of the DNA. The gummy candies represent the nucleotides. The reason you used four colors of candy is that there are four different types of nucleotides.

The special shape of DNA is called a double helix. On the outside of the double helix is the backbone that holds the DNA together. There are two sets of backbones that twist together. Between the backbones are the nucleotides, which are always paired. A different nucleotide connects to each backbone and then connects to another nucleotide in the center.

Did You Know?

Humans and cabbage share about 40 to 50 percent common DNA.

Did You Know?

About 99.9 percent of the DNA of every person on the planet is exactly the same. It's that 0.1 percent that is different that makes you unique and very special!

Brush an Egg

PREP TIME: 5 MINUTES PLUS OVERNIGHT
EXPERIMENT DURATION: 15 MINUTES

Supplies Needed
- ☐ Black permanent marker
- ☐ 3 clear cups or glasses
- ☐ Dark-colored soda
- ☐ Fruit juice
- ☐ Water
- ☐ 3 white eggs, raw or hard-boiled
- ☐ Toothbrush
- ☐ Toothpaste

Science Question:
Why is soda bad for teeth?

We will test what happens to teeth when we drink soda using eggshells as the stand-in for teeth.

The Experiment

With the marker, label one cup "soda," another "juice" and another "water." Fill each cup with the liquid you labeled it with. Place one egg in each cup and let them sit overnight.

In the morning, pour the liquids out of the cups, leaving the eggs in the marked cups so you can tell which egg soaked in which liquid. Examine the eggs to see how they have changed.

The Outcome

The egg in the soda, like your teeth, will become stained a dark color, and you might be able to see areas where the shell enamel is eroded and other areas where there are little pits in the eggshell.

Why It Worked

The enamel on your tooth protects the soft inside, or "dentin." When that is compromised or damaged, you will get a cavity (like the pits on the eggshell) and your mouth will begin to hurt.

Variation

- With a plain, dry toothbrush, try to brush the stains off of the eggs. Did they come off? Now wet the brush and try again with the toothpaste. See how important it is to brush your teeth!

Tip

For younger kids, try using a hard-boiled egg—less mess risk.

Did You Know?

In Japan, you can buy eel-flavored soda, called unagi nobori—yum!

Eye-Brain Tricks

PREP TIME: 15 MINUTES
EXPERIMENT DURATION: 5 MINUTES

Supplies Needed

- ☐ Cup
- ☐ Pencil
- ☐ Paper
- ☐ Scissors
- ☐ Markers or crayons (optional)
- ☐ Tape or glue
- ☐ Straw

Science Question: How smart is your brain?

Our brains are super smart: they can figure out information faster than computers can! In this experiment, you'll make a thaumatrope (a special toy) and see how your brain solves a "problem."

The Experiment

Use a cup to trace equal size circles onto your paper and cut them out.

On your circles, draw two pictures that share an element. For example, you could draw a goldfish on one side and a bowl on the other, or you could draw a bird on one side and a cage on the other. Make a "sandwich" of the two pictures and tape or glue the straw between them.

Hold the bottom of the straw and rub your hands to twirl the straw. What happens to the image?

The Outcome

When you twirled the straw, the two pictures blended into one!

Why It Worked

The pictures blended because of the persistence of vision. Your eye keeps a copy of the image or a memory of the image for $\frac{1}{20}$th of a second after the object is gone. As your toy spins, your brain interprets the series of quickly flashing images as one continuous image.

Variation

- Make a flip book. Use a small notebook and make a small image in the corners. In each image adapt it slightly from the previous image. We suggest using a dot, and each time move the dot. When you flip through the pages the principle of vision persistence makes it look like the dot is bouncing on your page.

Did You Know?

Your brain is 70 percent water!

Fingerprint Collection

MESS
METER: 2

NO ADULT
SUPERVISION
REQUIRED

PREP TIME: 10 MINUTES
EXPERIMENT DURATION: 10 MINUTES

Supplies Needed

- ☐ Hand lotion
- ☐ Glass cup
- ☐ Soft bristle paintbrush or makeup brush
- ☐ Cocoa powder
- ☐ Clear tape

Science Question:
How can you see fingerprints?

On our fingers are lots and lots of tiny wavy lines. These are fingerprints. In this experiment, we will make fingerprints on a glass and examine them, just like a detective might.

The Experiment

Rub some lotion on your hands. Grab the glass cup and try not to wiggle your fingers so your prints can be clean. Lift your fingers off the glass. Using the brush, dust a little cocoa powder onto the area of the cup where your hand was. What do you see?

Pick the best fingerprint and try to capture or transfer the print onto your tape by pressing the tape into the print carefully.

Why It Worked

The lotion on your hands soaked into the little crevices in your fingers, your fingerprints. Then when you touched the glass, the lotion transferred there. When you dusted your print with the powder, it stuck to the lotion. Voilà—visible fingerprints!

This is basically the same way detectives "dust" for fingerprints. The ridges on your fingertips have rows of sweat pores that constantly secrete perspiration. When you touch an object, that perspiration is transferred to the objects as a "print."

The Outcome

When you dusted the glass with cocoa powder, your fingerprints should have appeared!

Variations

- Instead of a glass, try transferring your fingerprints to other objects, such as a mirror. Can you get a fingerprint to stick to a rough object, such as fabric?

- Use ink on your finger to make a fingerprint on a balloon, then blow up the balloon to make your fingerprint super big.

Did You Know?

No one else has fingerprints exactly like yours. Even identical twins don't have the same fingerprints!

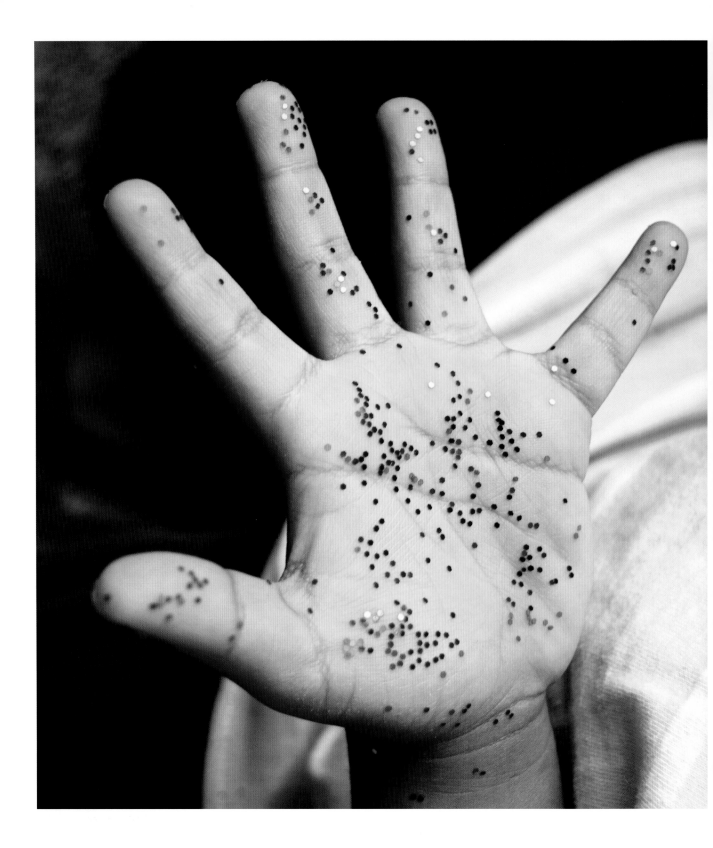

Glitter Germs

MESS
METER: 4

NO ADULT
SUPERVISION
REQUIRED

PREP TIME: 5 MINUTES
EXPERIMENT DURATION: 5 MINUTES

Supplies Needed

- ☐ Hand lotion (optional)
- ☐ Fine glitter
- ☐ Soap
- ☐ Paper towels

Science Question:
How do germs spread?

Colds, stomach bugs and flus are all caused by germs that are far too tiny to see with the naked eye; you need a microscope to see them. In this experiment, you'll use glitter to see how germs spread from person to person.

The Experiment

Put some hand lotion on your hands and rub it in. Then sprinkle some glitter on your hands. Rub them together to coat your fingers. Now, let's test how easy it is to catch your "glitter germs." Try the following tasks: Touch your nose. Shake your friend's hand. Wipe your hands off on your pants. Turn a doorknob. Did any glitter rub off?

Now rinse your hands with plain water. How much glitter came off? Next wash your hands with soap and water. Do another glitter check. Dry your hands with a towel. Is the glitter finally gone?

The Outcome

The glitter should have stuck to lots of things and been hard to rinse off with just water.

Try This!

Use your foot or an elbow to flush the toilet or open a closed public bathroom door. The handles in most public bathrooms have 400 times more germs than the toilet seat. Yuck.

Why It Worked

Just like the glitter was easily spread from person to person and object to object, germs are passed the same way. They hitch a ride on your fingers, and then they find their way into your body through your nose or mouth.

It is important to wash your hands after touching something that might have germs, such as when you use the bathroom or play outside. If you don't, the germs can easily spread to more places and to other people and cause sickness.

Variation

- Grab a spray bottle and pretend to sneeze by squirting your bottle (ah-choo!). Where did the spray go? Try it again only this time put your hand over your "mouth" (the spray bottle). See how less spray and germs escape when you cover your mouth?

Grow Gross

MESS
METER: 2

NO ADULT
SUPERVISION
REQUIRED

PREP TIME: 20 MINUTES
EXPERIMENT DURATION: 3 DAYS

Supplies Needed

☐ Spray bottle
☐ Water
☐ 1 teaspoon (5 g) sugar
☐ Loaf of bread
☐ Sandwich baggies
☐ Permanent marker

Science Question:
Where do we have the most germs?

Germs exist even though they are so small that you can't see them. In this experiment, we will grow germs found from our home—so we can see them.

The Experiment

Fill the spray bottle with water, add the sugar and shake the bottle until the sugar dissolves. Wash your hands and grab a piece of bread from the loaf. Spray it one time with the water. Then wipe the wet side of the bread on a surface in your house. Try the inside of your fridge, a doorknob, the inside of the kitchen sink, the toilet seat, etc. After you wipe a piece of bread on a "germ source," drop it into a baggie, seal it and use the marker to label the bag.

Put the baggies in a dark place to be undisturbed for a couple of days.

The Outcome

The germs from the wiped surfaces stuck to the bread and became food for the mold on the bread.

Variation

• Cleaning is important! Wipe a germy area with the bread and bag it. Then clean that surface and do a second bread wipe and bag it. A few days later, compare the two bags. How effective was your cleaning?

Try This!

To remove germs when you wash your hands, you should wash for 20 seconds. Think of a 20-second chorus and make that your "hand washing song."

Tip

Have an experimental control group; spray one piece of bread then immediately put it in a baggie without wiping it on anything.

Hole in Your Hand

MESS METER: 0

NO ADULT SUPERVISION REQUIRED

PREP TIME: 1 MINUTE
EXPERIMENT DURATION: 1 MINUTE

Supplies Needed

☐ Piece of paper

Science Question:
How does the brain translate what it sees?

Your brain fills in information and can jump to conclusions when there are gaps or differences between what we see and/or experience. Your brain can combine information it receives based on certain things you've seen in the past. Most of the time it's right, but sometimes your brain can be wrong!

The Experiment

Roll the paper into a tube. Hold the tube up to your eye and look through, keeping both eyes open. Lift up your hand with your palm facing you and move it closer to the end of the tube.

The Outcome

It might take a few seconds, but you will see a hole in your hand!

Why It Worked

Your left and right eyes see and send different visual information to your brain. Usually, both of your eyes see about the same thing, so your brain has no problem combining the left and right images. But this trick forces your left and right eyes to see images so differently that your brain can't blend them together correctly.

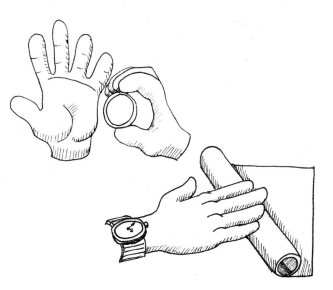

Try This!

Are you left- or right-handed? You probably know the answer to that, but do you know whether you're left- or right-dominant-eyed? Here's an easy way to find out. Wink! Which eye did you use? That's your dominant eye.

Lung Capacity

MESS
METER: 2

NO ADULT
SUPERVISION
REQUIRED

PREP TIME: 15 MINUTES
EXPERIMENT DURATION: 5 MINUTES

Supplies Needed

- ☐ Large, clean, empty plastic bottle
- ☐ Water
- ☐ Large container with a flat bottom
- ☐ Plastic tube or hose
- ☐ Masking tape
- ☐ Measuring cup
- ☐ Permanent marker

Science Question:
How much air can your lungs hold?

Air is vital for life. Our lungs are what fill with air as we inhale. In this experiment we see how much air our lungs can hold.

The Experiment

Fill your bottle with water and fill the large container half full with water. With your hand on the top of your bottle, turn the bottle upside down and set it in the container of water. Try to keep the water inside the bottle! Carefully put one end of the tubing under the water inside the bottle.

While a friend holds the bottle in position, take the biggest breath you can and blow out into the tube. Empty every last air molecule out of your lungs!

The Outcome

As you blew the air out of your lungs, down the tube and inside the bottle, the water level in the bottle went down. The water in the bottle was replaced with air. That is how much air your lungs hold.

Variation

- Measure how much air you have. Put some tape on the side of your bottle, from bottom to top. Measure 1 cup (235 ml) water and pour it into the bottle, then mark the tape. Repeat measuring, pouring and marking until the bottle is full. Do the experiment and see how many cups of air are in your lungs.

Try This!

Have a breathing contest! Who do you think has the biggest lung capacity? Compare lung volume between friends. Do bigger kids have bigger lungs?

Naked Eggs

PREP TIME: 5 MINUTES
EXPERIMENT DURATION: 3 DAYS

Supplies Needed

☐ Raw egg
☐ Glass container
☐ Vinegar

Science Question:
How do you make an eggshell disappear?

Eggshells are made of calcium carbonate. We can dissolve that shell, making the egg naked so we can see and touch the parts of a cell.

The Experiment

Place the egg in the container and cover it with the vinegar. Watch the egg for about 15 minutes—you should see bubbles form on the surface of the egg. Check the egg again after 8 hours and again after 3 days.

Why It Worked

The shell of an egg is made of calcium carbonate, which is a base. When vinegar, an acid, covers the shell it breaks down the calcium, releasing carbon dioxide (gas). You see this in the bubbles.

The Outcome

The eggshell will thin after about 8 hours and then completely disappear after 3 days. You can then see and touch the membrane covering the egg.

Variation

• If water hydrates, what does sugar do? Have two separate cups, one with water and another with corn syrup (the main ingredient in many sodas). Put an egg into each cup. After a couple of hours in the jars you can see how osmosis causes the egg in the water to get even bigger and how the sugars in the corn syrup dehydrated (pulled water out of) the other egg.

Super Sensitive

MESS
METER: 0

NO ADULT
SUPERVISION
REQUIRED

PREP TIME: 5 MINUTES
EXPERIMENT DURATION: 5 MINUTES

Supplies Needed

☐ Pencil
☐ Paper
☐ A partner
☐ Blindfold
☐ Cotton ball
☐ Paper clip opened up into a "U" shape
☐ Ice cube

Science Question:
What part of your body feels the most?

Did you ever wonder what part of your body feels and reacts the most? In this experiment, you will test your nerves and find out.

The Experiment

Using a pencil and paper, make a list of the places you will test on your partner, such as her arm, the bottom of her foot, her lip, her shin, under her arm, etc.

Blindfold your partner. Grab a cotton ball, paper clip and ice cube. Touch one item to different areas of your partner's body. Ask her to touch the spot where you touched her with the item.

Did she correctly identify the areas that were touched? If so, mark the chart. If she was "off" (even by ½ inch [1.3 cm]) from the exact location where she was touched, note that as well.

The Outcome

Your partner may not have identified all the exact spots where she was touched, or may have felt the paper clip more accurately than the cotton ball, for example.

Why It Worked

Our body has receptors in the skin to sense things, like cold, pressure or pain, and then send signals to the brain for a response. Some parts of our body do not respond as rapidly to cold or pain as others parts do.

Variations

• What happens if you touch two of those items on the same spot at once? For instance, can you feel both pain and cold at the same time in the same spot?

• Each touch receptor can send only one signal at a time. If two points touch the same neuron, it can still send only one signal to the brain. This means your brain will sense only one thing touching you, even when there are two.

Did You Know?

Nerve signals carry frequencies that are different for different reactions. A pain signal gets a faster response because its frequency is higher, so your brain sees that as an important signal requiring an immediate action to stop the pain.

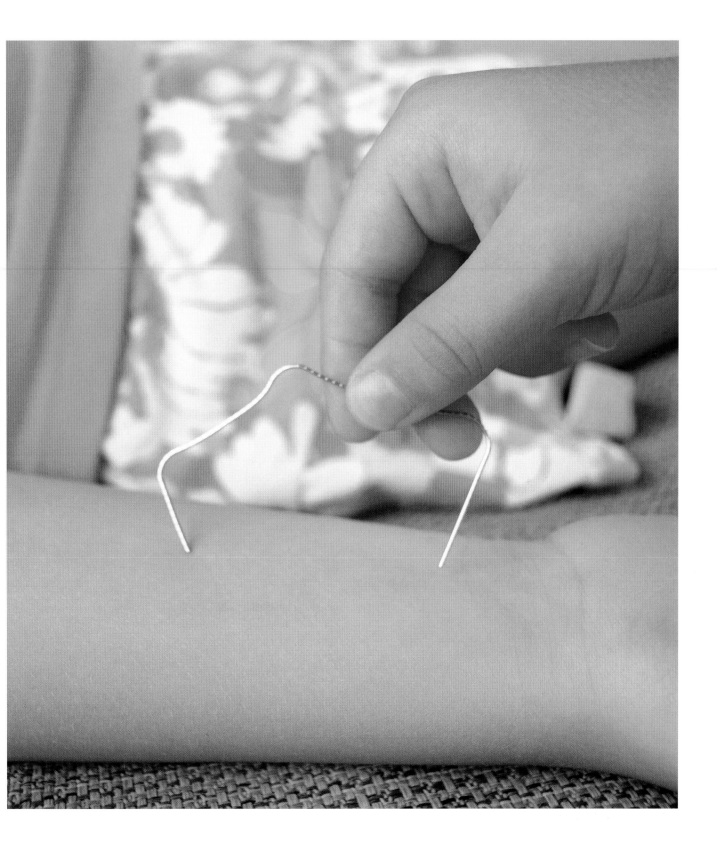

Paper Helicopters

MESS
METER: 2

NO ADULT
SUPERVISION
REQUIRED

PREP TIME: 15 MINUTES
EXPERIMENT DURATION: 5 MINUTES

Supplies Needed
- ☐ Ruler
- ☐ Scissors
- ☐ White piece of paper
- ☐ Colored construction paper
- ☐ Glue or tape
- ☐ Paper clip

Science Question:
How does the brain mix colors?

The primary colors are red, yellow and blue. With these three colors, you can make all the other colors!

The Experiment

Measure and cut the white paper into 3 x 8½ inch (7.5 x 21.5 cm) strips. Hold the paper like a hot dog and cut a slit through the middle of your sheet. These flaps will be your helicopter's "wings." Glue or tape two different primary colors of construction paper to each helicopter wing.

Attach a paper clip to the bottom, for weight, as shown. What do you think will happen to the colors of the blades when the helicopter spins? Bend the helicopter wings back so it looks like a "T" and give it a whirl!

The Outcome

When you toss the paper helicopter into the air, it should spin and hover for a bit. As the copter is spinning, the colors should mix together. So for instance, if your blades are red and yellow, they should look orange.

Why It Worked

The colors appear to mix because of persistence of vision. Your eye holds on to one image—for example, the red blade—while it is also seeing another image—the yellow blade. Then your brain combines the two colors, and you see orange!

Variation

- Add a fan that you can hold. Can you keep the helicopter afloat longer by pointing the draft from the fan at your helicopter?

Did You Know?

Leonardo da Vinci drew a flying machine in 1493. It took 450 years for a helicopter to be built and flown.

Singing Cups

MESS
METER: 1

NO ADULT
SUPERVISION
REQUIRED

PREP TIME: 5 MINUTES
EXPERIMENT DURATION: 10 MINUTES

Supplies Needed

☐ 3 glasses
☐ Water
☐ Vinegar
☐ Paper towels

Science Question:
What makes a sound?

Most of us hear sounds all day every day—so many, in fact, that we don't even think about most of them. But did you know sound is caused by vibrations?

The Experiment

Fill each of your glasses with different amounts of water. Dip a finger into the water and use the wet finger to make slow circles around the rim of each glass. Listen to the sounds each of the different glasses makes depending on how much water is in it.

Now wash your hands in a little vinegar and dry them with the paper towels so your fingers are really clean. Do you notice a difference in the sounds you can make?

The Outcome

Your glasses will sound much louder and cleaner after you clean the oil and dirt from your fingers.

Why It Worked

As you rub your finger on the rim of the glass, at first your finger sticks to the glass, and then it slides. This action creates a vibration inside the glass, which, in turn, makes a sound. Then those vibrations resonate together into sound waves, which you hear. As soon as the first few vibrations are produced, the glass resonates. You are making the crystals in the glass vibrate together and create one clear tone.

You probably noticed that the glasses with different amounts of water made different sounds and that you could make different sounds loud or soft by varying the pressure and speed of your finger.

When you washed with vinegar, besides your hands smelling like pickles, did you notice a change? Vinegar helps clean dirt and oil from your finger. A clean finger improves the stick-and-slide action that creates the vibration.

Variation

• Have friends and family fill glasses up with different amounts of water to make a musical symphony!

Water
Microscope

MESS
METER: 1

NO ADULT
SUPERVISION
REQUIRED

PREP TIME: 15 MINUTES
EXPERIMENT DURATION: 15 MINUTES

Supplies Needed

- ☐ Empty picture frame
- ☐ Something interesting to look at
- ☐ Dropper
- ☐ Water
- ☐ Magnifying glass

Science Question:
How does a microscope work?

A microscope is used to magnify small things to look larger so you can see them better. We will make our own microscope using a few things that can be found around the house.

The Experiment

Take the back off your picture frame and place your object under the glass. Add several drops of water to the glass over your object. This becomes your "lens." Hold the magnifying glass over the drops of water and move the magnifying glass closer or farther away from the glass until the object is in focus and easy to see.

The Outcome

The object will look larger through the water drop and the magnifying glass than it would have looked using the magnifying glass alone.

Why It Worked

You are using water to magnify objects. The water drops form the shape of a convex lens, which refracts light and converges it at the point where you can clearly see the image.

Did You Know?

This is how scientists created very early microscopes. Modern microscopes have lots of lenses and allow us to see extremely small objects.

Watch Your Pulse

MESS
METER: 1

NO ADULT
SUPERVISION
REQUIRED

PREP TIME: 10 MINUTES
EXPERIMENT DURATION: 3 MINUTES

Supplies Needed

☐ Toothpick
☐ Small marshmallow

Science Question:
Can you see your pulse?

Our heart is a muscle that works all the time pumping blood through our body. In this experiment we will watch our pulse, or the pumps, of our heart.

The Experiment

Put the toothpick inside the marshmallow so that it stands up by itself without being held. Place the marshmallow stick over the inside of your wrist.

Why It Worked

The artery in your wrist is very close to the surface of your skin, so that a very light object placed over it will move when the blood pumps through it.

The Outcome

Your pulse will cause the toothpick to waver or move slightly whenever the blood pumps through your wrist.

Variation

• Get a stopwatch and record how fast your pulse is. Now, do twenty jumping jacks and record your pulse a second time.

Tips

You can feel your pulse with just your fingers in your neck, just slide your fingers to the side of your Adam's apple.

Did You Know?

Your heart rate can vary between 60 beats a minute to over 200! It rises with exercise and is lowest while you're sleeping.

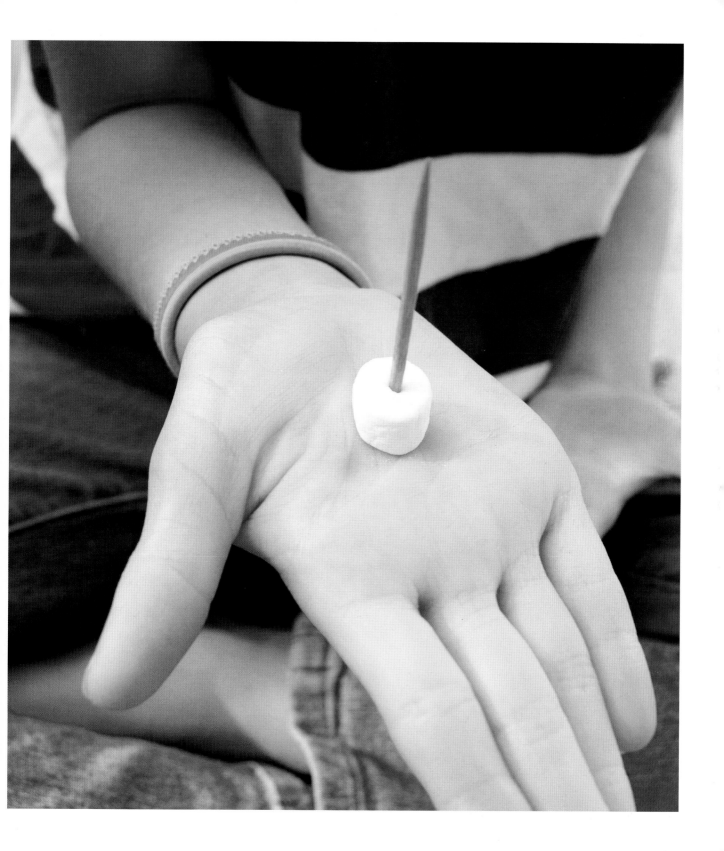

Bendy Bones

MESS METER: 1   ADULT SUPERVISION REQUIRED

PREP TIME: 10 MINUTES
EXPERIMENT DURATION: 2 DAYS

Supplies Needed
- ☐ Glass jar with a lid
- ☐ Vinegar
- ☐ Chicken bone

Science Question:
What makes bones hard?

Calcium is what is in our bones that makes them hard and strong. In this experiment we will see what bones would be like if they didn't have calcium.

The Experiment

Fill your jar with vinegar. Clean the meat off of your bone and put it into the jar. Put the lid on the jar and put it on the counter or somewhere where it will not be disturbed for a couple of days. After a couple of days, take your bone out and rinse it off (it will be slimy). Now try to bend it.

The Outcome

You can actually bend the bone.

Why It Worked

The acid from the vinegar breaks down the calcium in the bones, forming bubbles of carbon dioxide. When the calcium is gone, the bone has no hard structure to it, so it bends.

Variation

- Instead of soaking the bone in vinegar, bake it in the oven at 275°F (140°C) for at least 2 hours (have an adult help with this). Remove it from the oven and after it has cooled try to bend it. What happened?

Critical Thinking

Why is it important to have strong bones? What do you think you would look like if your bones were bendable?

Did You Know?

There are 270 bones in a human body when you are born, 26 of them are in a single foot. This means that over 20 percent of the bones in your body are in your feet!

Acknowledgments

Many thanks to the people who have helped make this book a possibility. At the top of that long list is Page Street Publishing. They have been a source of encouragement and problem-solving throughout this process. Page Street took a huge leap of faith when signing us up for our first book, *101 Kids Activities That Are the Bestest, Funnest Ever!* and have been the perfect partner for bringing our activities to print.

A big thank you to George Oosterhous and Aaron Warren for being incredible science resources. Their science students are blessed with instruction full of investigative learning. Their inspiration extends beyond the classroom walls.

We appreciate Josh Manges for illustrating this book. His ability to bring clarity to the steps that were stuck in our head was incredibly helpful!

Huge hugs go to our chief kid wrangler, Jana Stout, for her tireless work before and during photo shoots. She can also tell you where to get licorice in every color for the best price.

The kids! The kids! None of this could be possible without them. We adore them all and are so thankful that they are willing to play along during testing, re-testing and photos. Thank you to Halle, Rhett, Reid, Ryan, Noah, Jonah, Kora, Anya, Ezra, Lena, Mikayla, Jacob, Andrew, Peaches, Callie and Emma.

And last, but definitely not least, are our husbands. We appreciate the sacrifices made by Levi, Greg and Kevin. Their willingness to run out late at night on random errands, like a box of Borax or a nail with a certain metallic element, did not go unnoticed. We also promise that now the book is done, there is hope that every flat surface in the house can be cleared of science experiments.

About the Authors

The trio of authors have worked together on numerous projects, but as a team they are best known for Kids Activities Blog and the Quirky Momma Facebook page. Kids Activities Blog is the open-the-kitchen-junk-drawer-and-have-some-fun destination. They love kids activities that don't require special equipment or fancy set-up. The Quirky Momma Facebook page is an exhaustive resource for parenting, kids activities and family tips. The page grew over a million organic fans in one year due to its popular content. Today, this community is over 1.5 million fans.

Rachel Miller is a lifelong learner and educator. She is a specialist in nontraditional learning techniques and teaches classes in Integrated Chemistry and Art for grades K–8 and an Engineering class for grades 3–7 that uses only common office supplies as materials. She is a mom to a van-full whose favorite moments are exploring the world hands-on with kids. She is the creator of Quirky Momma and can also be found on her blog, One Crazy House.

Holly Homer is a retired Physical Therapist whose favorite subjects were Gross Anatomy and Chemistry. Her best summer was the one spent as a Gross Anatomy Lab Teaching Assistant where she was responsible for 40 students and 8 cadavers. She has served as a volunteer science teacher for grades 5–8 and now partially homeschools her three boys. She is passionate that learning shouldn't always include sitting. She can also be found writing the Kids Activities Channel on About.com, eBay.com and HollyHomer.com.

Jamie Harrington has loved science for as long as she can remember. She made her first model solar system for the third grade science fair, and still gets nostalgic for that bunsen burner smell in her high school chemistry class. In her kindergarten classroom, she always made sure her students spent more time working hands-on with science so that they could really know how things work. Teaching kids real-world applications for science is really important to Jamie; she loves doing science experiments with her daughter and is super jazzed about sharing what she knows with a new generation of learners! Jamie also writes for the *Huffington Post* and her blog, Totally the Bomb. Her work has appeared on Yahoo, BuzzFeed and Condé Nast.

Index